CW00735143

THE BOOK OF THE BIVVY

ABOUT THE AUTHOR

Since his antique Saunders Jetpacker went porous in 1996 Ronald Turnbull has stopped bothering with a tent. He has made six bivvybag crossings of Scotland coast-to-coast and slept on sixteen Scottish summits: twenty-four English, three each in Wales and Northern Ireland and one on the Isle of Man. He writes regularly for *TGO*, *Lakeland Walker*, *Trail* and *Cumbria* magazines. His previous books include *Across Scotland on Foot*, *Long Days in Lakeland* and *Welsh 3000ft Challenges*. He has written one other Cicerone guide, *Walking in the Lowther Hills*, with another, *Walking in the Cairngorms*, in preparation.

Winner of the Outdoor Writers' Guild's Award for Excellence – Best Outdoor Book 2001

The OWG Award judges described the book as 'Quirky. Entertaining. Funny. Heart warming. Very well researched and stunningly presented.'

THE BOOK OF THE BIVVY

by

Ronald Turnbull

© Ronald Turnbull 2001
ISBN 1 85284 342 X

Reprinted 2004

A catalogue record for this book is available from the British Library.

DEDICATION

To the man in Ruigh-Aiteachain bothy who asked: "but what happens if it rains?" I'd walked a long way that day, and it didn't come out very lucidly. But the answer's disarmingly simple, and he'll find it in Chapter 5.

SAFETY NOTE

A survival bag or bivvybag, carried as an emergency shelter, is a valuable safety aid.

However, when the bivvybag is used in place of a tent on trips through wild country, the margin of safety is reduced. This practice is only recommended to those with hillwalking experience, who understand the use of map and compass and how bad the weather could get. The normal precaution of leaving a timed route-plan with a responsible person is even more important for bivvybag walkers.

Cover photo: Summit bivvy on Sgurr nan Coirechan, Glenfinnian

CONTENTS

FOREWORD

by Julian Miles
designer and manufacturer of
Kathmandu Trekking bivvybags and bashas

When Neolithic man and Neolithic woman first slipped quietly into a cave, stopping only to build a fire at the entrance before disappearing inside for a long, long weekend, humanity gained a sense of privacy, but began to lose touch with its environment. This process has been going on ever since.

Within a few days, two pairs of eyes began to look out over the flickering flames, into the sunshine and the darkness, at the forests and the hills, as the wind blew, the snow fell and the rain lashed the rocks. Those eyes had already begun to forget what it was to be out there all the time, with the animals, at the mercy of the elements, and probably even more vulnerable than the wolves and the deer were themselves. Then one day there were three pairs of eyes looking out, and man had a home, a family to look to, and little time to remember what it had been like…

A lot of water has passed under the bridge since then, much of it very murky water indeed. But throughout the world, except in areas where shepherds still sit and watch the sheep, or the plough scrapes through the soil behind an ox, people look to the land, whether it be called heath, highland, outback, wilderness, savannah, desert or jungle, with an ancient longing to return, albeit temporarily, to what was before.

There are many ways of doing it. From the Mongolian nomad sheltering in the luxury of his felt-clad yurt against the gales that tear across the Steppes to the wretched tin boxes some people drag around behind their cars from one campsite to another.

In between we have the ageless 40-pounder tent that can hold a platoon of soldiers, the conviviality of the patrol tent of the scout and those metal-framed contrivances that take all evening to assemble. Then there is the greater portability of the ridge tent, and the later geodesics with their flimsy aluminium flex-poles, whose versatility allows the creation of a profusion of shapes, sizes and designs in myriad colours.

But these are, one eventually gets to realise, still structures. A compromise can be achieved by stretching a basha above a sleeping bag. But this is another structure, and a draughty one at that.

And then, needs spawning deeds, there is conceived and brought forth a home that can be taken from a rucksack, unrolled, thrown to the ground, and climbed into in an instant, in any weather, anywhere, any time.

Thus the bivvybag was born.

In this book Ronald Turnbull takes us through every aspect of bivvying, from our shepherd wrapped in his fleece, and later strange practices on mountains, through the novice with his appalling and nearly useless orange plastic bag, to the variety of cheap-to-expensive breathable bags on the market.

Within these chapters appears a strange race of people. The small, sinewy mountaineers of the 19th century, who seem to have approached their mountains with little foresight or planning and consequently suffered the death-rate of wartime pilots; and later, the hard men with frost in their eyelashes, rainwater in their underwear and tiny rucksacks on their backs, pounding the hills like demented grape-treaders determined to get it done as rapidly as possible...

Now this, dear Reader, is bivvying *in extremis*. It is quite possible to take your bivvybag onto the lawn on a spring evening, with a cup of cocoa and a candle, and have a wonderful time; or to escape to the hills with a 60-litre rucksack packed with wholesome food, and spare woolly socks, for a three-meals-a-day warm and dry wander with your chums. The strange thing is, however you do it, you still end up amongst the streams and the trees, the tumuli and the dolmens left by the ancient peoples, whose world you share as you walk and sleep with your bivvybag.

This is not a conventional handbook, packed with dreary facts and figures, mostly irrelevant, about bivvies. That stuff is to be found on the swing-tickets in the retailers' shops. But it does take you through the history of, and equipment used by, people who have bivvied and who bivvy now.

Then it is up to you either to sit back and dream, or go out and do...

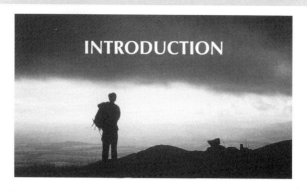

INTRODUCTION

'Exploring is delightful to look forward to and back upon, but it is not comfortable at the time, unless it be of such an easy nature as not to deserve the name.'

Samuel Butler – *Erewhon*

Ah, Knoydart! That remote peninsula is reached by no road, but by a long ride up the West Highland Railway and Bruce Watt's boat out of Mallaig. Leap onto the jetty at Inverie with a real feeling of anxiety and self-reliance. The boat won't be back for two days, and it's 30 miles to the bus stop.

And those miles aren't easy ones. Knoydart's rough bounds are well separated from the so-called Real World, concealed in mists and snowclouds, defended by midges and the mysteries of the ferry timetable. Here the sea creeps deep into the hills, the hills drop steep into the sea – and eight feet of water a year are transferred from the one to the other in the shape of rain.

Knoydart in the rain is where Hamish Brown came closest to abandoning his All-the-Munros walk. Get lost in the mist and it's 600 metres down a vertical bog, and what you get at the bottom is a river in spate and no footbridge.

It's best, here, to expect anything at all in the way of weather. And when a surprising sun beats down out of a sky of blue – as it does not infrequently at all in the month of May – we were equipped to cope. In my sack was a small green Gore-tex bag supplied by an elderly but very lively member of the Scottish Mountaineering Club. In Oliver's sack was a similar one, and in his head the route-plan for this very eventuality.

Sgurr na Ciche. It's the hard heart of the Rough Bounds. Its rocky sides steepen as they go up, till its top contour lines crowd so close there isn't even space for a spot height. By the side of Loch Nevis we stopped to brew a simple supper, and looked at the Ciche. Its western ridge started as a seaweedy spine rising out of the loch; indeed, its rocky outline could be seen plunging on downwards into the salt waters. Sun-heat beat back at us off the rock spine, the warm air carried the aroma of the bog myrtle, and the bees were buzzing around in the heather. Assuredly not a night for the bothy.

Knoydart's Rough Bounds, Sgurr na Ciche on right

And so we raced the setting sun up the three miles (and one vertical kilometre) of the ridge. All the way the pointed summit stood like a beckoning finger against the sky. We scrambled on hands and knees up the final steep metres to reach the cairn in time for the last two minutes of the day. The sun went down behind the rim of Ladhar Bheinn like an egg yolk falling into the blades of a liquidiser.

At this point we may calculate the altitude of Heaven as 1042m (3418ft). For on Ciche's summit, at sunset, it is within touching distance.

Two minutes down the eastern sides we found, among all the bare schist, a grassy shelf sheltered by lumps of crag. Twenty miles away Nevis, that urban hill, crouched under the stars. All night long our noses poked into the night and were cooled and freshened by the breezes.

But by dawn those noses were damp ones. Grey rain had rolled in off the Atlantic. Tendrils of cloud swirled around our little hollow; we were annoying damp tealeaves to be scoured out of its pristine sink. We bundled up the bags and dropped 800 feet to warm up before breakfasting huddled under a wet stonewall.

Julian Miles calculates that he's made about 8000 bivvybags over the years, not to mention the more expensive but perfectly serviceable products of his competitors. Where are they all?

Is it just that the bivvy is so discreet that we don't see it? A gentleman who didn't give his name spent four months in his one, watching a farmhouse in Kent where some thieves were preparing to steal the great De Beers diamond from the Millennium Dome.

But are the other half-million or so bivvybags manufactured by Britain's lively outdoor suppliers all simply sitting in attics and their nervous owners taking them out every six months or so and saying, do I quite dare? Or don't I? Like English lasses on a Spanish beach wondering whether or not to go topless...

Head of Loch Nevis, below the long ridge of Sgurr na Ciche

Topless – topful – topping – over the top – there's a pun here, struggling with its zips and trying to emerge into the open air. So far the bag has mostly been taken up by serious long-distance types, and of course the Special Forces. But even on a simple tropical beach sleep-out, it does make all the difference not to have the morning dew joining you in bed. Or take a bottle of whisky to the first flat place above the youth hostel and join Prince Charlie in the heather.

They are the best of nights: they are the worst of nights. The modern lightweight tent has opened up the wilderness – but for an increasing number of people, the lightweight tent is just a bit too civilised. Can you really experience nature's rawness from inside a zipped-up storm-flap? For those who want to bring a bit of old-fashioned pain and suffering back into the outdoor experience, the bivvybag is the place to be.

In a tent you have to unbag, boot up, and crawl all over a sleeping companion to see what the stars are up to. In a bivvy, the stars are shining right down onto your nose. When the moonlight falls onto a sea of cloud, and the Isle of Skye floats across the sea like a silver dream, do you really want to be zipped up under a green dome asleep? And when the wind howls in the heather and the rain gradually trickles in, you don't experience the full misery when you recline in waterproof tented splendour. If you like to travel a nice short distance with a comfortingly heavy pack, and to spend the sunset hours lying in a cramped green space rehydrating little packets over a cooker, then what you want is a tent. Or perhaps a youth hostel, or hotel. But if you want to walk right across the Lakes in a weekend, or right across Scotland in a week – if you prefer a small portable rucksack with no oppressive luxuries (like Karrimats, dry clothing, or cookers) to interfere between you and the mountain experience – then you want the little green bag.

Apart from anything else, a tent won't ever fit onto that ledge of Sgurr na Ciche.

My thanks to various companions (Oliver, Colin, Virginia and Glyn) for confirming that it's not just me, and that the bag really is for having fun in. Julian Miles carefully explained just why I'd got so wet in Belfast, and has given useful advice on various technical points. Don't waste their efforts. Find a sunset summit somewhere and shake out that bag.

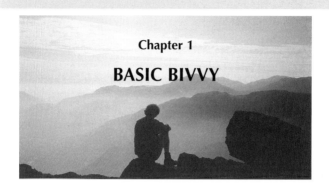

Chapter 1

BASIC BIVVY

PEIGNE AND SUFFERING

On the way up, we met two other British people coming down. 'Benighted: abseiled off: you'll see our rope hanging in the chimney.'

Silly Brits, don't understand Alpine climbing, always get benighted. We'd pick up their rope as we passed it and bring it back to the campsite that evening. Or that late afternoon – the Aiguille de la Peigne is one of the smallest of the Chamonix Aiguilles, good rock and Grade III (British Diff) all the way.

The trouble with guidebooks is that they're written by people who are very good at it. Our book was an English-language selection. The English-language selectors had omitted the Ordinary Route up the Peigne in favour of this terribly easy but rather nice rock route. But there are 600m/2000ft of that terribly easy rock. This is fine if you consider English Diff a scramble and climb it unroped. It's not fine if you consider English Diff a climb.

As we went up we looked at our watches, looked at the rocks above, and got less and less British and more informally Alpine in our climbing. We reached the previous people's jammed rope and removed it from the chimney. We got to the top of the climb and crossed onto the ordinary route. We abandoned all idea of the summit and set off down the ordinary route. It got darker.

The trouble with downhill rock climbing in the dark is that you can't distinguish the worn footholds, the trampled ledges, the turned-over screes of the correct line. So on a suitable rocky ledge we decided to stop and get benighted.

All night long we heard the meltwater dripping, so the temperature can't even have got down to freezing. And we were equipped. We'd read all about it in *The White Spider*, and we'd gone in to get some of this sophisticated survival equipment. 'I would like,' I told them at Tiso's, 'a bivouac sack.'

They looked puzzled, then laughed. 'Ah – you mean a polybag!' Surprisingly for such an advanced bit of kit, the cost was only five shillings.

The five-shillingsworth were bright orange and rather thick. I wriggled into a cosy hole below some boulders. The other people's rope, coils opened out into a long figure-eight, made a bed that was almost comfortable. A barley-sugar sweet, placed in the downhill cheek, spread an illusory warmth – bad for the teeth but good for morale. I certainly slept for some of the time.

After we'd listened to about a hundred thousand drips, the dripping darkness gave way to a dripping grey half-light. When you know you're about to leave the bag and be even colder it seems less uncomfortable. A good shiver warms you up and then you can doze a little. Until a strange whirr and sudden rattle from overhead...

We were directly underneath the Mont Blanc cablecar. Fifty yards away in the grey air, well-fed people were passing through the sky in a warm plastic box. Their windows were steamed up: with any luck they couldn't see us.

We packed our bags and scurried down the mountain. In the meadows below, the first of the new day's climbers were heading for the Peigne. A pair with the patched-breeches look of the British were heading off towards the bottom of the 600m/2000ft terribly easy rockclimb...

PROBLEMS OF THE POLYBAG

Today we've upgraded the name to 'Survival Bag' but the price is relatively unchanged at between £5 and Free With This Month's Issue. And there's no doubt that these things do aid survival. Dumfriesshire, for example, has two extra inhabitants because of them. An elderly neighbour suffered a mild heart attack in the Enterkin Pass and lay for five hours in a snowstorm. A much younger one fell while descending into Glen Shiel, broke both ankles and jawbone, and nobody knew where he was except a friend who'd just that day emigrated to New Zealand. He lay in his bag for four days.

No piece of equipment does better in terms of lives saved per pound sterling, with the possible exception of bootlaces and other short lengths of string. But the survival bag means what it says. You wake up miserable, but alive.

Much of that misery is down to dampness. A medium-sized human, in the course of a night, emits about a pint of water. This pint (or half-litre, for a slightly smaller person who thinks in metric) condenses on the inside of the plastic. From there it gets into your hair, your clothes, your sleeping bag if you're lucky enough to be in one. It gets in between the pages of this book: the later chapters will be largely concerned with that pint of water in the night.

The plastic sort of bag is like the western side of Scotland. It's warmer, but also wetter.

This book is about misery that's mixed in with pleasure, rather than taken straight: about self-indulgence rather than mere survival. However, all bivvybags do have a secondary function as survival aids, and it's true that you can't have much of either fun or suffering if you died the previous winter.

For pure survival, there are various items offered of lightweight plastic or so-called 'space blanket'. These cost very little, weigh very little (about 100g/3oz) and they're very little use.

That's not the same as no use at all. After the London Marathon they gave us aluminised plastic wrappers with the sponsor's logo. Thus we became, among the streaked concrete of Waterloo Embankment, a fluttering blue and silver throng as we consumed an other-worldly sports drink which itself tasted strongly aluminised. Space blanket claims to conserve 90 per cent of body heat. This is misleading. Heat is transferred by radiation, conduction and convection. When lying under a stonewall in a snowstorm, heat is lost by conduction (into the freezing ground below) and by convection (into the passing breeze above). Aluminised plastic reflects only radiant heat.

However, when strolling on the Embankment damp with sweat and wearing only your undies, the blue and silver wrapper is what you need over damp skimpy shorts and a Galloway Sheep tee-shirt.

This wrapper came free – I only had to run 26 miles to get it. And while it was of little use, it was also of little weight, which could be good value; so I took it on the Mountain Marathon. On these events a cooker is compulsory: so I also brought along some delicious savoury rice. Alas! When Glyn unwrapped the cooker it was of a purely formal sort – small paraffin blocks, a stove like a dead spider sculpted out of rust, and a foil tub for saucepan. The super-lightweight saucepan had been remarkable value: less than £2.50, with its first hot meal, plus beansprouts, included at no extra charge. However, it had been on several mountain marathons already and was no longer rice-tight.

Ideal bivvybagging in the Picos de Europa, Spain

A saucepan liner cut from the London blanket turned out to be just the thing. It shrivelled above the soup-line, but held below. The moral? Anything's useful, so just take whatever weighs least…

However, for serious survival (which means survival of snowstorms) you need a serious survival bag and this weighs 300g/10oz. This is thick enough to hold in heat as well as air, and stiff enough that the breeze won't mould it against your body. The books say you should bite a hole in the corner of it to breathe through and then enter it head first. This makes sense: warm air rises and stays in the bag. However, I've never been quite desperate enough to bite a hole in something that cost me five shillings.

Two are not twice as warm as one in a bag, unless the bag's a very big one. If the bag gets tight it compresses your clothing and the bits of you pressing against the outside get very cold indeed. There are, however, group bags: these are specifically designed for several people to get miserable in together.

PLASTIC BAG FOR PLEASURE PURPOSES

Some of us are too mean to buy a proper bivvybag, and some of us just like to see how much we can do without. I come into both categories. So here is the technique for primitive plastic travel.

If plastic bags get wet on the inside, the way to stay dry is to stay outside the bag. A foam mat is one of the things you probably didn't bring, and the double layer of plastic underneath is insulation of a sort as well as groundsheet.

When it starts to rain, you can postpone the damp by moving under a nearby tree. When the rain starts to drip through the leaves, it's just possible it may already have finished raining outside.

Otherwise, it's time to get into the bag. Position it with the feet end slightly uphill. This means that condensation in the bag has a chance to trickle out the entrance. It also means that raindrops on the outside will drip off the doorway rather than trickling back inside. If you hold the entrance well open, air can get in and evaporate some of the condensation.

You wake up moist but warm. It's the next night, the crawling back into a bag that's already damp, that's going to be really horrible. So the advice is not to do that next night, but to head off the hill to civilisation with its youth hostels and shops selling proper breathable bags.

However, it may quite possibly not rain at all. In which case you simply keep going until you run out of muesli. You lie late to let the sun take the dew off the plastic, amble down to the village whose lamps had lightened your night-time, and discover that, late though you lay, it's still two hours too early for the shops.

POLYBAG FACTS

- The basic polythene survival bag should cost between £5 and nothing at all – they may be given away free with outdoor magazines. A fertiliser sack does the same job more cheaply, though the bedtime reading printed on the outside is less entertaining. (The new big-bag style is a good size: it's important to wash out all traces of the previous contents as fertiliser damages the skin.)

- The more the bag weighs the more effective it is – but the more it weighs, obviously. Eight to twelve ounces is a good balance between heaviness and uselessness. It should be long enough to be able to get right inside with boots on, and fold down the end so as to let the rain drip – this means 2m/7ft. If planned for two, it should be big enough to hang loose around them rather than stretched tight about their bodies.

- The multi-person shelter does offer a significant weight saving, quite apart from the conviviality. The three/four person 'Windblokka' weighs 600g/1lb 4oz and is made of proofed ripstop nylon. It costs about £45. It's designed for sitting up in rather than lying down and going to sleep.

One night under the moon in a plastic bag should persuade you that you want more nights under the moon, but in something other than damp plastic. Rawhide? Potato sacks? Stout Harris tweed? In the next chapter we'll study various historic bivvybags even less accommodating than polythene.

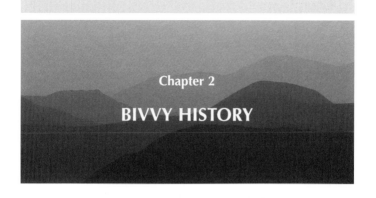

Chapter 2

BIVVY HISTORY

Brian an augury hath tried
Of that dread kind which must not be
Unless in dire extremity,
The Taghairm called; by which, afar,
Our sires foresaw the events of war.
That bull was slain: his reeking hide
They stretched the cataract beside.
Crouch'd on a shelf beneath the brink,
Close where the thundering torrents sink,
Midst groan of rock, and roar of stream,
The wizard waits prophetic dream...

The period from 1900 to roughly 1969 was a dark age of outdoor technique.

When the Marathon was reintroduced as an Olympic sport a hundred years ago, it was considered unnecessary and unsporting to drink water along the way. As a result, Marathon runners tended to collapse and die at the 20th mile. Certainly, 26 miles and 300 yards were too far for all but the toughest and most athletic: too far for the entire female sex. Today, 30,000 people every year cover the distance, some of them only moderately fit, some of them dressed as chamber pots and crocodiles. And at every mile marker they pass a drinks station. But we can be sure that Pheidippides, who was the original Marathon runner, knew about the importance of water. So did the Aztec post-runners, who covered over a hundred miles a day up and down the Andes.

When the Dyhrenfurth expedition attempted Kanchenjunga in 1930, each expedition boot, once its massive crampon was strapped onto it, weighed in at 2.85kg/6lb (5.7kg/12lb the pair). Professor Dyhrenfurth seems to have considered this a good thing, as it strengthened character along with legs. And yet the Roman soldier, as he padded along the ridge of High Street, knew all about lightweight footwear. Legionaries wore hob-nailed leather sandals; auxiliaries preferred the lightweight boot called *caligula*. One report describes the *caligula* as very comfortable, and better than the modern military boot. The upper was cut from a single piece of leather, laced all the way up the front and sometimes left open at the toe and heel. The sole-pattern resembled that on a modern pair of trail shoes – designed to optimise the distribution of the walker's weight. Today's boot design may just about be catching up with the Romans. It would be interesting to run a comparative gear test against a pair of Brashers…

Back in the dark days of 1970 I headed up into Glen Affric for a week of Munro-bagging. On my back was the state-of-the-art rucksack: a dangling pear-shape of stout canvas. Any self-respecting Roman soldier would have flung that pack into the bog. It added 10lb to the effective weight. And that effective weight already included the tent of the time: 11lb of cotton, and hemp cordage, with wooden poles connected with ferrules of solid iron. The 33 pegs on their own weighed more than a tent of today.

And yet, 100 years earlier, imaginative Britons had been sleeping out under tents with a total weight, including poles and groundsheet, of nothing at all. In 1878, the writer Robert Louis Stevenson appears to have invented the bivvybag.

'This child of my invention was nearly 6ft square (i.e. before sewing into a bag)… a sort of long roll or sausage, green waterproof cart cloth without and blue sheep's fur within.

A tent, above all for a solitary traveller, is troublesome to pitch, and troublesome to strike again; and even on the march it forms a conspicuous feature in your baggage. A sleeping-sack, on the other hand, is always ready – you have only to get into it; it serves a double purpose – a bed by night, a portmanteau by day; and it does not advertise your intention of camping out to every curious passer-by.'

So here is bivvy-literature's first recorded night out in a bag. Like many after him, RLS leaves it rather late to select his bedroom...

'The rain had stopped, and the wind, which still kept rising, began to dry my coat and trousers. "Very well," thought I, "water or no water, I must camp."

The wind roared unwearyingly among the trees; I could hear the boughs tossing and the leaves churning through half a mile of forest; yet the scene of my encampment was not only as black as the pit, but admirably sheltered...

I tied Modestine [his donkey] more conveniently for herself, and broke up half the black bread for her supper, reserving the other half against the morning. Then I gathered what I should want within reach, took off my wet boots and gaiters, which I wrapped in my waterproof, arranged my knapsack for a pillow under the flap of my sleeping-bag, insinuated my limbs into the interior, and buckled myself in like a bambino. I opened a tin of Bologna sausage and broke a cake of chocolate, and that was all I had to eat. All I had to wash down this revolting mixture was neat brandy: a revolting beverage in itself. But I was rare and hungry; ate well, and smoked one of the best cigarettes in my experience. Then I put a stone in my straw hat, pulled the flap of my fur cap over my neck and eyes, put the revolver ready to my hand, and snuggled well down among the sheepskins.

I questioned at first if I were sleepy, for I felt my heart beating faster than usual, as if with an agreeable excitement to which my mind remained a stranger. But as soon as my eyelids touched, that subtle glue leaped between them, and they would no more come separate.

The wind among the trees was my lullaby. Sometimes it sounded for minutes together with a steady even rush, not rising nor abating; and again it would swell and burst like a great crashing breaker, and the trees would patter me all over with big drops from the rain of the afternoon...

When I awoke for the third time, the world was flooded with a blue light, the mother of the dawn. I saw the leaves labouring in the wind and the ribbon of the road; and, on turning my head, there was Modestine tied to a beech, and standing half across the path in an attitude of inimitable patience. I closed my eyes again, and set to thinking over the experience of the night. I was surprised to find how easy and pleasant it had been, even in this tempestuous weather. The stone which annoyed me would not have been there, had I not been forced to camp blindfold in the opaque night; and I had felt no other inconvenience, except when my feet encountered the lantern or the second volume of Peyrat's Pastors in the Desert among the mixed contents of my sleeping-bag; nay, more, I had felt not a touch of cold, and awakened with unusually lightsome and clear sensations.'

But even earlier, in 1858, the explorer Charles Packe was backpacking across the Pyrenean High-level Route, and sleeping out on the summits of Lakeland.

He spurned the mountain *cabanes* of the shepherds (a lodging which few Englishmen would prefer to the open air).

'Throughout the chain, and especially on the Spanish side, there is a great deficiency of hotel accommodation on the mountains, so that a sleeping bag is almost an indispensable part of his kit to anyone who would see and thoroughly enjoy the grander parts of the Pyrenees... More may be seen in the mountains in four or five days' camping out than in three weeks of hotel life with an occasional excursion. Besides the bag, a tin saucepan with a lid, a frying pan and a few spoons ought to be taken.'

According to Packe's obituary, there was hardly a mountain top of eminence in Britain on which he had not passed the night, often with no shelter but a blanket or a cloak. His companion Count Henry Russell-Killough used the mountain itself as his bivvybag. After digging several caves into the side of 3298m/10,824ft Vignemale, he had himself buried overnight at the summit. His head alone stuck out into the clouds, and frost formed in his beard.

But whatever we think of the rival claims of Packe and Stevenson, it's clear that the mystic exploitation of the bivvybag goes back much further than either of them. The quotation at the head of this chapter is from the 4th canto of *The Lady of the Lake* by Sir Walter Scott. This 70-page poem has 30 pages of notes to it. Helpfully, Sir Walter explains:

'The Highlanders, like all rude people, had various superstitious modes of inquiring into futurity... A person was wrapped up in the skin of a newly-slain bullock, and

Informal bedroom of the fifth century: St Ninian's Cave at Whithorn

deposited beside a waterfall, or at the bottom of a precipice, or in some other strange, wild, and unusual situation, where the scenery around him suggested nothing but objects of horror.'

Although Scott doesn't say so, it seems clear that the subject should lie naked within the warm and bloody hide, with only his head showing. Leather is moderately breathable – that's one reason why it's good for making boots with. However, it probably is not as good as Gore-tex or Milair, if we judge from the contemporary records.

'One John Erach of the Isle of Lewis was a night within the hide; during which time he felt and heard such terrible things, that he could not express them; the impression that it made on him was such as could never go off, and he said, for a thousand worlds he would never again be concerned in the like performance.'

Much has been written about the North Face of the Eiger (in German, Eigerwand) – in the 1930s the most dangerous and difficult face in the Alps. In the first four years of attempts none succeeded, and of the ten who set foot on the face, all but two lost their lives. (For comparison, of every 30 people who climb higher than Everest Base Camp, four reach the summit and one dies on the mountain.)

What is less frequently realised is that the eventual conquest of this face was down to advances in bivvy technique.

The early attempts fell into a pattern that soon became familiar to the watchers at the telescopes of the Grindelwald hotels. Fit and vigorous, the climbers would make excellent progress on day one, crossing the first icefield and even the second before being pinned down by the afternoon stonefall. They would then bivouac. After the bivouac they would continue much more slowly, hesitating at every difficulty. They would make less than half the height gain of the previous day and be forced to a second bivouac. On the third day they would vanish behind the clouds of an Eigerwand blizzard, and some time later their bodies would be found in the avalanche cone at the foot of the face.

Most famous of the Eiger overnight spots was at the top corner of the Flatiron buttress, between the Second and Third Icefields. This small stance under an overhang, sheltered from stonefall, became known as the Death Bivouac. The first seven to sleep here either died of exposure and exhaustion or were caught soon afterwards by storm or stonefall; the eighth, the Italian Corti, only got away by being winched off the Traverse of the Gods by a climber who descended 1,000 feet from the summit on a wire cable. The bivouac was again used on 28th August 1961 by Adi (Adolf) Mayr, attempting the first solo ascent. He climbed very strongly to reach the Flatiron early on his first afternoon, but was brought to a stop there by stonefall. The next morning he was seen to climb with unaccountable hesitancy and slowness, and fell to his death from the Ramp.

The discovery that was the key to the face was not the famous Hinterstoisser Traverse but rather the bivouac site immediately above: the Swallow's Nest. Here it is described by Heinrich Harrer (all quotations are from his book *The White Spider,* translated by Hugh Merrick).

'We reached our rock knob and were able to fix two belaying-pitons; then we spent hours in digging a small seat out of the ice below it. We tied ourselves and our belongings to the pitons for security's sake, furnished our seat with coils of rope, and started to cook our meal. The knob of rock afforded us complete protection from stones; the view from our perch was magnificent. All the conditions for a happy bivouac were present...'

At this bivvy, in 1962, Chris Bonington used as a bivvybag the plastic cover of Hamish MacInnes's motorbike. Coming across another climber who needed rescuing they abandoned their attempt without much regret – a bike cover isn't an adequate bivvybag at 2500m (8200ft).

It was an Austrian climber called Ludwig Vörg who discovered this Swallow's Nest, level with the bottom corner of the First Icefield and protected by an overhang. Its comforts allowed the climbers to start the second day refreshed, and to cross all three of the icefields before stonefall.

Not for nothing was Vörg the 'Bivouac King' (Bivakkonig). He equipped the Swallow's Nest with fleece-lined sleeping bags and airbeds, and built it a low wall of stones. And as the ascent unfolded, his bivouac technique was crucial. The four climbers spent their second night on the Ramp, below the Waterfall Chimney (the 'usual bivouac place, a good bivouac').

'We arranged our bivouac about 8ft below that of Heckmair and Vörg. We managed to drive a single piton into a tiny crevice in the rock. It was a thin square-shafted piton. It held after only a centimetre, but it was just jammed.

Obviously, once we hung our whole weight on it, it would very likely work loose with the leverage. So we bent it downwards in a hoop, till the ring was touching the rock. In this way we did away with any question of leverage and knew we could rely on our little grey steely friend. First we hung all our belongings on it and, after that, ourselves...

We managed to manufacture a sort of seat with the aid of rope-slings, and hung out some more to prevent our legs dangling over the gulf. Next to me there was a tiny level spot, just big enough for our cooker, so we were able to brew tea, coffee and cocoa.

Heckmair and Vörg were no more comfortably lodged. The relaxed attitude of Vörg, the 'Bivouac King', was quite remarkable; even in a place like this he had no intention of doing without every possible comfort. He even put on his soft fleece-lined bivouac-slippers, and the expression on his face was that of a genuine connoisseur of such matters. It is absolutely no exaggeration to say that we all felt quite well and indeed comfortable... Our perch was about 4000 feet above the snowfields at the base of the precipice; if one of us fell off now, that was where he would certainly finish up. But who was thinking of falling off?

It was a good bivouac.'

On the third day the weather, as usual on the Eiger, got very bad. Their final bivvy was above the White Spider, in the Exit Cracks.

'After we had climbed an ice-bulge, we came upon a rock-ledge protected by overhangs from falling stones and avalanches. When I say a ledge, I do not mean a smooth comfortable feature on which it is possible to sit; it was far too narrow and precipitous for that. Heckmair found a place where he could drive in a rock-piton firmly, and with great patience fixed enough hooks on which to hang all the stuff, as well as securing himself and Vörg. Fritz and I arranged our overnight abode about 10ft away. The ledge was scarcely as broad as a boot, and only just allowed us to stand erect, pressed close against the rock; but we contrived to knock in a piton to which we could tie ourselves. Even then we couldn't sit, not even on the outer rim of the ledge.

However, we found a solution. We emptied our rucksacks and tried fastening them too to the piton, in such a way that we could put our feet in them and so find a hold. We were sure it would work all right, and so it did.

Between us and our friends we had fixed a traversing rope, along which a cookery-pot went shuttling back and forth. Vörg had taken on the important post of expedition cook… Fritz, being Viennese, is a coffee connoisseur, and praised Ludwig's concoction…

It was now 11pm. Ludwig had given over cookery and "retired to rest". Even here, on this tiny perch 12,300ft up, and 5000ft sheer above the nearest level, he hadn't foregone the comfort of the bivouac-slippers. Andreas had to keep his crampons on, so as to get some kind of stance in the ice for him to maintain a hold; but his head rested on Vörg's broad back… Fritz and I had pulled the Zdarsky-sack over us; our rucksack architecture served splendidly as support for our legs, and very soon I could hear the deep, regular breathing of my friend as he slept by my side. Through the little window in the tent sack I could see that there were no stars in the sky and the weather was still bad; it looked as if it were snowing. There was an occasional small snow-slide from above, but they only slid over the skin of the tent, with a gentle swishing sound, like a hand stroking it... I wasn't worried about the weather. I was possessed by a great feeling of peace; we would reach the summit tomorrow. This sense of peace increased to a conscious glow of happiness. We humans often experience happiness without recognising it; but here, in that bivouac of ours, I was not only genuinely happy; I knew I was.

This, the third bivouac for Fritz and me on the North Face, was the smallest in terms of room; in spite of that it was the best. And if you ask me why, the reason was the rest, the peace, the joy, the great satisfaction we all four enjoyed there.'

Harrer's book not only gives a detailed description of the route, but the all-important data on the various bivouac sites, from the Bivouac Cave, above the shattered pillar and below the Difficult Crack (narrow and wet; too low), to the 'Comfortable Overnight Spot' to left of the Ramp icefield – first used by Rébuffat and French members of the European ascent of 1952. Ludwig Vörg himself was killed fighting on the Russian front in 1941.

This Eiger expertise was slow to spread to the flatlands. Even in the comparative humpiness of the Scottish Highlands, the hard men were wrapping themselves in groundsheets, or constructing howffs out of heather and stones in the hollows below various dripping boulders. But all that was about to change.

In 1938, William L Gore discovered Teflon and started wondering what it was for. 'Teflon' (which is a registered trademark) is the lightweight name for polytetrafluorethylene. In the 1960s men started going to the moon. In the process they discovered that Teflon was useful for non-stick saucepans. In 1969 Bill Gore's son Bob Gore was playing with a sheet of Teflon and discovered that if he stretched it suddenly in both directions, it grew billions and billions of tiny holes.

The Age of the Bivvybag was about to begin.

Chapter 3

THE BREATHABLE BAG

FIVE NIGHTS IN GREEN PLASTIC

1 Overnight Ochils

You can't find more suitable hills to walk in moonlight than the grassy Ochils. No need to use torches on these easy slopes, and the views are even better in the dark because of the lights. The Ochil valleys are deep holes of darkness, and a great orange sea of sodium light stretches away to the south.

We unrolled bivvybags in a grassy canyon between two hills, with a small stream trickling somewhere. Here we lay in a floating bowl, looking out and down at the cities of the plain.

The thistles were so comfortable we overslept till 5am. The water bottles froze in the night and so did we – but it didn't matter about the water bottles as mine had been left lying downhill, so the ice was all at the end where the little lid wasn't. Dawn crept up from behind, warming the fingers and sculpting the hills with rounded light. The Forth valley was all mist, with oil refineries sticking up like island castles; their chimneys poured wide white stripes across the morning. Vapours ebbed and flowed like slow thoughts in the mind of a giant whose alarm clock hasn't gone off yet.

There's a certain incentive not to get up – it's literally freezing out there. On the other hand, it's also very cold here in the bag, and the only way to get warm will be to get moving. We'll eat once our fingers thaw.

Weak sunlight gleamed on the distant Firth of Forth and on us. Four hours into the walk, we met our first fellow-walkers. And down in civilised Stirling at lunchtime, it was quite a surprise to find overnight ice still knocking about in the water bottle.

2 Wet Wooler in November

The green undulations stretching dully to the horizon; the solitude; the wet bedclothes – I'd be a single-handed yachtsman if I could pay for the boat. As it is, I must make do with the not terribly dry land of the Southern Uplands. A crossing of the bottom of Scotland in November offers every important feature of the solo transatlantic except seasickness.

Walking in the dark does strange things to the mind. After an hour of stumbling through mud, 7pm felt like the middle of the night. I was, on my eventual return to houses and electric light, to suffer from jetlag. The map ahead said, 'stream, plantation; high valley walls' – in other words, *bedroom* – and the map didn't lie. I unrolled the bivvybag on a voluptuous bed of pine needles below the branches.

In November, if nights are clear they're unbearably cold; otherwise it rains. This was one of the warm wet ones, so I slept for quite a bit of the time. In the expensive sort of bag, you zip yourself into a featureless green slug-shape the same at both ends, and alarm innocent householders when they wake to find you on their lawn. My bag is what it says: a simple bag. So it was necessary to wake up every hour to drink the water in the entrance before it flowed over the doorstep.

Untroubled even by thirst, then, I lay listening to the drips till six in the morning before setting off through the drips to look for the Cheviots.

3 Hoover Bag

On a May evening in 1994, I lay between two tufts of heather, 450m/1500ft above the town of Callander, immediately below a vivid sunset in green and orange stripes. A lump of hill blocked off the cold wind out of the north – it also blocked off the leaping skyline of Stuc a' Chroin and Ben Vorlich.

Those Munros didn't matter. My eyes and thoughts were fixed on two peaty lumps to the south. Uamh Bheag (pronounced, very roughly, hoover bag) lies south of the geological Highland Line and is therefore a Donald, though not listed in the tables as such. And I was about to attempt a record-breaking 10-day run over all 148 of those small southern Scottish hills.

Before a long run, it's important to get a good night's sleep. The heather was scented and dry to lie on, the sunset was soothing. Wind whispered through miles of surrounding grassland. I pulled the sleeping bag tight around my face and closed my eyes.

My morning preparations were simple. Two of Mr Kipling's apple pies, eaten in bed with gloves on. Shoes on, roll up the bag, and away. First hilltop 10 minutes later, at 5.07am; start the stopwatch and start running. Only another 147 to go…

4 Man Management

An island is simply a ridgewalk with the sea at each end and also on both sides.

A motorbike can get right round the Isle of Man in 18 minutes. On foot there's more to it than several very sharp bends and some cattle-grids painted gorsebush orange (not just to match the actual gorsebushes, but to make it slightly easier not to crash). I had a day in hand for the spine of the island, and the spine of the island is 33 miles with several hills in.

But the aeroplane doesn't leave till 11am. A bivvybag dawn would give not just a sunrise over the sea but five hours of morning to walk through. And a bivvybag rucksack makes 33 miles not at all too much for a day and a dawn and a morning.

So with a shop's worth of pork pies and bananas in the bag, six or seven hills behind, and a pale mauve sort of sunset on the right, I walked southwards towards the toe of the Man. The waves were too far down to hear, even though there was no wind; but the low sunbeams bouncing off the ocean showed the shoals and cross-currents in swirls of alternating shiny and black. A twiggy scent rose off the heather on one side, a cool draught off the sea on the other. Black choughs wheeled in the fading air. I stopped on Bradda Hill to watch the end of the day. Would the last sunbeams flash through the seawater horizon in the mystic phenomenon of the Green Flash?

No, silly. The Mountains of Mourne are over there; and two inches above the sea, the sun slipped away behind a jagged horizon. I wandered up the still visible path, heather brushing bare legs, and found a fallen wall with a view of the last daylight and also eastwards towards the dawn of following morning.

The heather was deeper than blankets, and scratchy against the green nylon of the bivvybag, like two-day stubble. Ears cooled in the night air below the woolly hat, but everywhere else was warm as I ate the bananas and the pork pies and watched the sea go purple. Then I leant back and went to sleep.

Bike and bivvybag: heading onto Cross Fell

5 Saddle Bag

The day had not been easy. Silly you feel, sitting behind a bicycle on a station platform for two hours waiting for a train that's late. And on the cyclepath from Whitehaven, strong wind in the face, then strong wind and rain, then strong wind and snow. I came down into Keswick cold and slow, the brake blocks screaming as if in severe pain.

And then came the Old Coach Road – considered as the challenging option, but what hadn't been considered was ice in the puddles and snow over the top. March sun shone on the high face of Blencathra, sky was blue as lark's eggs, and cycling was exciting through puddles well over the pedals.

Whereupon, at five in the evening, it all suddenly stopped being difficult. A downhill swoop, and a short climb to warm up with, and another downhill swoop. Air like iced vodka, and a sort of drunken vigour that just wanted to keep pedalling rather quickly on and on into the night. Which I could, as I hadn't booked. And I didn't have to book, as I had a bag to fall back into.

Just as well I did have the bag. The first wayside inn was sorry but it had no spaces left tonight. Maybe if I'd had a respectable VW Passat purring in the car park, maybe if I'd had mud-free legs and something on those legs that wasn't pale blue Lycra… The second wayside inn had no spaces left tonight, sorry.

But in the little pinewood near Penrith there was plenty of space. I leant the bike against a fallen tree, and shone the front lamp around to find if there was anything in the wood I wouldn't want to lie down on. The pine branches shut out the glimmer of the stars, but even so there was a suspicious crispness about the pine-needles. The motorway sounded a lullaby rumble and beamed night-lights between the tree-trunks. I wriggled under the fallen tree to save some of my night heat from the emptiness of the night sky.

It may have helped a little. My trainers, well wetted along the Coach Road, froze stiff during the night. I had to wear them on my hands for 10 shivering minutes before they would yield and let my feet in. Four miles downhill into the town was a bitter bit of riding, but 120m/400ft of climb let me re-establish communication with my toes. Next night, halfway down the long downhill to Sunderland, I swung off early to a bed and breakfast.

They gave me some sheets of newspaper to undress on.

A bivvybag in some modern breathable fabric keeps away the rain but lets out most, or even all, of the condensation. It costs between £50 and £200 – later I'll discuss whether you want to spend the smaller or the greater sum. Fifty pounds is the price of two nights in a hillwalker's hotel, or five in a bunkhouse. For £200 you could join the Scottish Youth Hostels Association for about 50 years.

Alternatively, your £200 could get you a little tent. In your little tent you could cook suppers, undress indoors, and lie till 9am reading this book.

On Sgurr nan Coireachan at sunset (Chapter 6)

Sunset summit: Kirriereoch Hill, Galloway, view to Arran

A bivvybag may not be all that expensive, but it's not a way of saving money. It is, rather, a new way of having fun. A bivvybag isn't simply an extra bit of kit that has the backwards effect of making the rucksack lighter. It's a new attitude, a new way of being in the hills. It rearranges the co-ordinates of space and time and allows us to wriggle through the wormholes into a different universe.

TIME, THINGS AND MIGUEL

Time

Time is a tyrant. How often in a day do you look at your watch or the clock on the wall or the clock on the town hall? Ten minutes to catch the bus, two hours to knocking-off time…

Even on the hill, there's the four hours until it gets dark and the three hills we want to get over before. There's the bed and breakfast that expects us at seven, and the train we're wanting to get at Achnashellach next Tuesday. A timepiece is as necessary for safety as will be, all too soon, the mobile phone. And in each case the outdoors is coming slightly closer to the office.

Time may be a benevolent despot – as when you've started at six instead of nine, walked into the evening, and got yourself half a day ahead. Pleasant and lazy are the days that are half a day ahead, but then you spoil it all by deciding you could actually catch that train on Monday rather than Tuesday. And there you are again, half a day behind, pressing forward up every hill, irritable at every shut shop or unnecessary cup of tea, cross because the sun has come out on the summit you left 10 minutes ago but you're certainly not going to go back for that photo…

A bivvybag is the thing that lets you do without things, and one of the things that you could do without is a watch. Dispense with the timepiece and get – paradoxically – more time.

Wander watchless until the sun sets, find another sleepy hollow and go to sleep in it. Will tonight be the one that rains and sends you back down into the real world where they wear watches? You can cross the whole of Wales this way if the sun shines. For me the wet night came on the Fforest Fawr; next morning I dropped off the ridge to the roadside wondering what day of the week it was.

On ordinary hill days you need to know when you're going to get benighted. With bag that doesn't matter. Walking watchless is one of those simple pleasures whose appeal is – obviously – timeless. It's also one of those pleasures (like bivvybagging itself) that's not altogether pleasant. For the first day you keep glancing at your wrist and worrying. Not knowing what time it is is a new level of insecurity and freedom. There's no day's target to achieve or fall behind when you don't know when you are at the moment. There are more interesting things to think about than whether you can grab back five minutes on the ascent of Waun Fach.

But time doesn't give in so easily. Can you keep right on to St David's without ever knowing how late it is? Or will you fall back into the valleys and have to stop at a clock?

Things

You can spend many interesting hours deciding what items to buy, and many slightly less interesting ones earning the money. But, disappointingly, your fellow walkers aren't going to go Gore-tex green with envy at your cool new bivvybag.

This is because the bivvybag is the item that encourages you to get rid of other items. You've saved 2kg/4¹/₂lb on the tent; why not save a bit more by not taking the cooker? The bivvybag attitude tends to disobey the Consumer Imperative. It doesn't bother to shave, and keeps warm under many thin layers of worn-out stuff it should have thrown away four years ago. As you get further and further from the car park, the breathable jackets get shabbier, the hats are bobble instead of fleece, the boots are scratched and old. Four hours out you meet the breeches. Eight hours out it's the rucksack fixed with string. And on the furthest, loneliest hilltop, as the stars come out, is the chap or lassie in the bag.

For this is the thingless thing, the genuinely money-saving purchase. By its aid you climb the Hill Difficulty into the Cloud of Unknowing.

Also, by the time you unroll the nice new bag, everyone who could have admired it has cleared off down to the pub.

Diogenes the Dog

A bivouac is defined as any form of shelter less than a tent. It could be breathable Sympatex, it could be sheepskin, or it could be a woollen plaid. The only timber bivvybag on record was inhabited by Diogenes the Cynic in the third century BC. He had to, as he was 2400 years before Gore-tex.

The timber bivvybag hasn't ever caught on, but Diogenes is still the founder of bivvybag philosophy. The treasures of this world – flashy jackets, walking poles, the satellite GPS navigator – cause only grief and envy. The absence of a marble palace or a flexible-pole domeline tent may be more enjoyable than the proud possession of it. Sadly only two lines of dialogue from this original master have come down through the ages. Alexander the Great came to visit the barrel. 'Hi,' he said, 'I'm Alexander the Great.'

'And I am Diogenes the Cynic.'

A nasty smell came from inside the barrel. The bed appeared to be a pile of old rope. 'Ah – ahem. As the greatest emperor in the world so far, is there anything I can do for you?'

'Yes there is,' said our hero. 'Could you shift yourself a little bit to the side? You're standing in my light.'

While on a sea voyage Diogenes was captured by pirates and sold as a slave in Corinth. He was purchased by a rich man who found him amusing. But you don't have to be rich to buy a basic Milair bivvybag.

You just have to find it amusing.

Miguel

The bivvybag, if it were alive, would be a Spanish mountain guide called Miguel. Miguel has eyebrows like thorn-scrub and a hat that has no shape whatever. Even if you could see in behind his black and grey beard you wouldn't find any facial expressions.

Miguel looks at my nice new rucksack (dynamic posturing adjustable strapwork) in a way that makes me wish I'd walked a couple of thousand miles under it before letting him see it. He walks slowly behind at the beginning of the afternoon, and 2000m/6500ft of hot contours further up, but half an hour below the hut, overtakes at the same slow speed.

That hut is dark and timber-lined, recalling the interior of the barrel lived in by the Greek philosopher. The table is a massive plank, wine appears in a battered aluminium flask. Outside, a mountain like a 1000ft tombstone – the Naranjo de Bulnes – is going bright pink all over. And Miguel speaks. 'You will have the common cheese? Or you will have the *Cabrales* cheese?'

Now this is important. Is the Cabrales a joke? Or is it some form of ordeal? Or is it, simply, a cultural gulf between different racial tastebuds? The Cabrales when it arrives is mouth-shrivellingly awful, blue-brown in colour and tasting of goats and sump oil.

And the reason this is important? Well, when I come back from dropping the Cabrales off a handy precipice outside the hut, Miguel will speak again. And he will say, with a vague gesture upwards, 'Tomorrow, for us, the Naranjo de Bulnes.'

Joke – ordeal – or simply a jolly nice day on the mountain?

Chapter 4

MIDLEVEL BAGGERY

'I followed a flight of steps down to the vegetable plots on the
river bank. Under a wild cherry at the water's edge I unrolled
my sleeping-bag. As the light faded I dined from a tin of
mussels, mopped up with stale bread, and familiarised myself
again with the noisiness of night. The river roared, insects
sounded like aeroplanes and the occasional "plop" of a cherry
falling on my sleeping-bag felt more like the impact of an
apple dropped from a cliff-top. Then there was that primitive
fear of being found, alone and defenceless in sleep. I drove
Que Chova [his umbrella] into the meadow grass by my head,
within easy reach.'

Nicholas Crane, *Clear Waters Rising,* in Galicia, Spain
(Penguin Books 1997)

CAVE BEHAVIOUR

A soggy Sunday in October, and men in tracksuits are taking orange
markers off Raven Edge after the weekend's hillracing. Down at the
Kirkstone, cars are draining from the car park in synch with the light
draining from the sky: in each case leaving behind a wide and
somewhat stony-grey emptiness.

But at the Kirkstone Inn they bravely serve Sunday lunch until it's
time for Sunday supper. Above Colin's head is a picture of the winter
drifts and intrepid motorists with shovels. In another couple of months
this is going to be a lonely place.

In another couple of hours, indeed, this is going to be a lonely place. Around us as we tuck into our carrots and roast, the tables gradually empty. With brown emptiness indoors and grey emptiness outside, sticky toffee loses its attraction. Besides, we don't want to haul half-digested sticky toffee up Red Screes. There are three hills to cross and a cave to find, and two and a half hours of day to do them in. We climb briskly up Red Screes, with only the pimpled footprints of the fellrunners for company.

Up on top it's cool and very quiet. The hill looks scruffy with its fallen walls and wide trampled paths. But mankind has retreated behind the walls of its cities, leaving Red Screes to whatever creatures roam the night hours. In this case, to Colin and me.

We wander over Little Hart Crag, and follow broken fencing up into the cloud. On Dove Crag we come across the trodden road of the Fairfield Horseshoe, the artifact of a vanished race and civilisation. Crag should be vertical, but the top of Dove Crag is flat stones in the mist, and a wall leading forward. But then we drop out of the col, drop out of the cloud, and find Dove Crag the Crag.

It's been said that if you fall off the top of Dove Crag you go down 90m/300ft without touching rock and land 6m/20ft out from the crag foot. I haven't tried it myself, and it really doesn't look any worse than vertical. It faces north, so stays damp all day, and the strata are all wrong so there's no handholds. Thus, in the 10 years 1955–65, Dove Crag turned from the nastiest, most unclimbable cliff in Lakeland into a sporting and amusing bit of rock covered in juicy routes.

No holds, but one very notable hole. Somewhere in the top right-hand corner of all this is the Priest's Cave. It isn't visible from below; you reach it by a climb or scramble above 90m/300ft of sporting and amusing, and we had 25 minutes to find it or sleep on the wet hill.

We discovered a path leading up into the crags, but it just came out at the top. We found a ledge leading across, but it just ended in the middle. And then Colin came upon a little rock stairway worn grey and pale, and a footpath zigzagging up. No wet hill for us tonight.

The cave is a wide black slot with a low, badly-built wall across it. Inside there's almost enough room to stand up, and a floor of beaten earth. The bedrock sticking up out of the floor is a bit low for sitting on, but worn smooth by many boots and bottoms. The floor is excellent. With a foam mat below the bivvy, its small stones will be almost comfortable; more important, they aren't going to poke holes in the expensive Gore-tex. And at the back there's a tin box containing various practical items: a broken umbrella and some metal mesh for the fireplace; a vodka-bottle candleholder; two delicately scented blankets and the visitors' book.

Outside there's a few feet of gravelly ledge, a balcony for sitting and contemplating the evening. The evening is ordinary – cloud just above, and rain all around the horizon – but the balcony view makes it special. Below are a few yards of steep grass and then the valley floor 300m/1000ft further down. A single light shows from the Brotherswater Inn, but the rest of the scene is grey shading to black.

Just as the light goes, the rain arrives. We retire to the interior to cook and read the book.

It's the Priest's Cave because a priest may have sheltered here but probably didn't. However, in the intervening years it has housed priests, mullahs, lamas and those of no spiritual persuasion whatever but just a well-formed silly streak. An inch of visitors' book has been written in less than a year. They were here at the Millennium Moment, found it rather cold, and watched snowflakes blowing upwards past the entrance and fireworks at Penrith. Some friends of Colin were here when they should have been mending a bothy somewhere in Scotland. Fourteen people from Outward Bound were here, along with three adults. Steve complained of the lack of reading matter in the metal box, the two Daves complained of the distance to fetch water, Ruth complained of the need to pee, Graham from Walsall advised against sleeping next to the wall. But most found that the combination of the situation, the damp paper, and the dried-up biro reduced them to a few incoherent words.

A small waterfall of drips was splattering onto the ledge outside. Tendrils of mist wafted through the blue light of the Coleman. I went to the entrance to see the lights of Penrith – and saw a huge black figure lurking in the air. A Brocken Spectre, twice life size, was thrown onto the mist by the candle at my back...

I stood for three minutes, arms outstretched, while the camera tried to take a long exposure of my spectre. But the spectre was shy, and the film shows only black.

We slept well, lulled by the splattering of the raindrops a few feet away, the cool draught over our noses and the fragrance of the blankets. We lay late till half-past seven, shook the tealeaves into the abyss and 30 minutes later were standing on the top of Fairfield. A shaft of sunlight caught us on Cofa Pike, Grisedale Tarn slopped around vaguely in the mist, and we came down Striding Edge in rain that puddled in the gaps in the rocks and streamed down the handholds. Coming off the ridge we encountered a human or two, and down by Lanty's Tarn they were pottering around in plastic macs, poking at the mud with orange walking poles. 'Are you really enjoying yourselves?' they asked us.

With the Priest successfully slept in, Striding strode, and the car just 10 minutes away across the river, we had no trouble in saying we had been.

Finding the cave from above

The path down into Dovedale doesn't follow the 'Public Footpath' line on the OS map. (Instead it leaves the low point of the col and goes down the valley bottom past the small tarn at GR374111.) Follow the PF line rather than the path, descending alongside Dove Crag. The cave is not visible from below (unless on Hartsop above How with binoculars). It is at the top of the vertical part of the crag, altitude 670m/2199ft. Look out for a 5ft easy scramble, leading to a terrace path – this scramble is at 650m/2133ft (for those with altimeter). One zigzag above is the cave. Note that the scramble is undemanding (except when it's icy), with good holds and well worn. If you are on dodgy adventures among vertical rocks, you are certainly in the wrong place.

The cave remains dry in most winds. There's no water closer than the Dovedale path except after heavy rain. The scramble is just difficult enough to deter sheep.

The floor is trodden earth with small stones in it; a foam mat is strongly recommended. The place is occupied on most Saturday nights.

FALLBACK BAG

You're going to buy the bag, at the end of this chapter, for those mid-summer sleep-outs on the Carneddau. But the simple fact of having the bag allows expeditions to remote caves in winter. If night should fall with the cave undiscovered, it's nice not to have to lie out and die of exposure. Equally, it'd be a pity to lug up a tent and find the pegs won't go into the rocky floor.

The unused bag comes into its own again on bed-and-breakfast journeys. The disadvantage of such journeys is that they tie you to a schedule. If it's fine, you may be wanting to do two days at a time, or divert into the mountains. If it isn't, you may want to linger a day and put all the washing through the tumble-drier.

When its too wet for the bag, the bothy: when the bothy's burnt down, back into the bag. Riugh-aiteachain in Glen Feshie

With a bivvybag, you can leave B&Bs unbooked. Turn up where you want, and if it's really nasty one of the people who booked won't have turned up. So the odd night when you end up in the bag will very possibly be the nice-weather one.

Scottish bothies are romantic nightspots. However, sometimes you arrive in the dark to find you can't find the bothy. Or it may be burnt down, or full of really unpleasant people; or the Mountain Bothies

Association has moved in and taken the roof off. A bivvybag in the rucksack means not having to worry about the bothy.

Foreign parts

With a few exceptions, such as Iceland, the climate of Abroad is just right for bivvybags: warm or pleasantly cool at night, with bursts of heavy rain followed by nice hot sun to dry out again. Whenever I've taken a tent to foreign parts I've always wished it was only a bivvy.

Dry out between bag nights at a bunkhouse:
Carrour Station on Rannoch moor

Even on civilised low-altitude holidays, you never quite know whether the bus is going to take you to the right place. It's a comfort to have your own green breathable bedroom.

The one difficulty may be finding out in advance about mosquitoes. The bag I took to the Picos de Europa lacked midge-netting, but above 1000m/3000ft it didn't matter. And I did end up feeling over-equipped: Spanish rockclimbers were using foam mat and sleeping bag only.

SHOPPING FOR BAGS

What bag you want depends on what sort of shopper you are. Do you like to have the best and are you prepared to pay for it? My own disreputable principle is to buy the second-cheapest. If it should fail me, then at least I know what I need next time.

A featureless bag costing £100 or less will keep you alive through the storm, and keep you enjoyably alive on beach sleep-outs and fine-weather mountaintops. It packs down light and small. When the mountaintops start to become a habit you may decide you need something a bit bigger and thicker. Then when they say you're crazy up there, you can lend them the old bag and make them try it for themselves.

1 Plastic bag

See Chapter 1 for suggestions for polybag best buy (or best pick-up at field corner).

2 Basic bag

For many years I have been using the Milair bag from Kathmandu Trekking. This weighs in at 400g/14oz and costs around £45. Its only feature is a drawstring closure at the top end. Milair is rather less breathable than Gore-tex. On the other hand, it is a great deal less expensive. For a long time this was my only bivvy, and I still use it when I don't expect severe weather overnight, as when sleeping on Lakeland summits, and for long-distance treks when weight really matters and nasty nights will hopefully be spent in bothies, bunkhouses or B&Bs. I have come across no other bags as light and inexpensive, so KT seems to have this end of the market to itself.

3 Pertex bag

Rab make a Pertex bivvy which is as cheap and light as the KT one (the Survival Zone, 450g/8oz, £50). It is superbly windproof and breathable. It is tough, withstanding the rigours of the cave floor. However, it is only moderately waterproof.

4 The slightly bigger bag

The more serious bag I use is the Discoverer from Terra Nova (650g/1lb 7oz, £100 if you're lucky; manufacturer's recommended retail price £130). TN call this their 'entry-level' bag but for me the silage sack is entry level and this is expensive luxury. This is rather larger than the KT basic bivvy, and has a waterproof plastic base. These two aspects go together – KT does make a less expensive bag with a thicker layer underneath, but as the bag is rather small it rolls over when you do, taking the underlayer to the top and spoiling the point. The TN bag stays the same way up; and now the waterproof underside really does make sense. It's tough, and less likely to stop being waterproof when it meets thorns or pebbles. It's easy to clean. It's slightly cheaper. And you're not going to breathe into the damp ground, so what's underneath doesn't need to be breathable.

The other new feature at this level is the broad zip across the top, which creates a half-separate hood end. This can be closed completely during downpours, and unzipped a little at either end for normal damp nights. On fine nights you bring your head right out on top of the hood to enjoy the moonlight, with none of the usual business of trying to keep the nylon stuff off your face. The hood is also useful at breakfast time – place it over your head and gain a huge sheltered area in which to eat sandwiches, darn socks and study maps while the rain drips directly onto your knees.

At this weight and price I have found the TN bag completely satisfactory. I've no reason to believe that bags from other manufacturers such as Vaude are any less good – I just haven't been inside them in any thunderstorms. The TN happened to be the second-cheapest in the shop I went into. The next most expensive has a midge net entry, which could be useful if sleeping low in Scotland in summer.

5 Fancy bags

Manufacturers always ask which features we would like, and they all seem quite likeable. They don't ask, would we like to pay an extra hundred pounds sterling and carry an extra one pound avoirdupois? So now we get bivvybags with extended head ends for rucksacks; internal poles (though in fact the humble KT has loops for a willow-twig to create a ventilated bell end); even pegs. What you end up with isn't an extremely luxurious and comfortable bivvy – it's an extremely cramped and uncomfortable tent. One such weighs 1.25kg/2lb 12oz, and at £249 even the price is tent-like. Compare the Vaude Scorpion, which is a single-skin two-small-man tent at 2.05kg/4lb 8oz and £250.

I have never owned or used one of these 'luxury' bivvies. So it's only my prejudices that are telling me that it's another case of paying more to spoil the point. But don't they look silly in the campsite with their owners passing the evening in their cars alongside?

6 How big a bag?

A bag is too small if it's stretched tight across any part of you. The sleeping bag below will be compressed, and a squashed bag doesn't have any warmth. This is only likely to happen if you are a particularly large person (or perhaps two people) in the bivvybag.

If you're tall and like to sleep with your legs straight, make sure the bag is long enough. It needs to come right over your head, without pulling, and flop down beyond to let the rain run down.

After that it's simply a matter of how much space you like to have around you. A bag with a cheap non-breathable base should be big enough to let you roll over in your sleeping bag while keeping the underneath of the bivvybag underneath. A roomy bag has more trapped air inside it but this doesn't affect its warmth or performance very much.

A generously-sized bag can weigh, and cost, twice as much as one that's small but not too small.

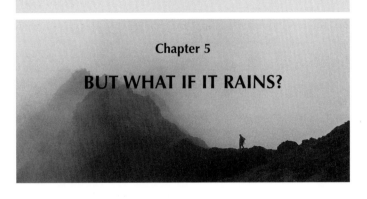

Chapter 5

BUT WHAT IF IT RAINS?

'Man is born to suffer, and you especially.'

Leopold von Sacher-Masoch, *Venus in Furs*

WET UNDER THORNS IN BELFAST

It had rained, and it was going to rain. After three fine far-seeing nights on the summits of Mourne, I was in for a wet one. Time to look for a place with a roof.

But this was Northern Ireland, where the walking is unwalked. Youth hostel? Well yes, two days behind or a day and a half ahead. Camping barn? Not on the edge of Belfast. So I started trying the places listed in the Ulster Way guide. £50 single room – in a walkers' listing: golly. Next one: £60. Then a small bed and breakfast in a side street wanted to know where I was from.

I was a bit clueless here. I should have announced confidently, 'I'm from Scotland and I'm an atheist, Madam.' Instead I mumbled something about being on the Ulster Way, and she hoped I'd enjoy it but she was full.

But above the city are the Belfast hills: basalt covered in heather is an excellent bed, with a sea view over streetlights. What could be nicer?

Well, the people of Northern Ireland are very friendly. They slow their cars beside me, slip clutch alongside for 10 minutes so as to talk to the walker, are genuinely pleased that a Scottish atheist wants to hike to the Giant's Causeway, and discuss – in a concerned and friendly way – the Belfast Hills. I should get myself through them before the marching season, and I should get myself through them before dark. Statistically, non-Irish come to arbitrary harm less often here than we would in Glasgow. But two who did were murdered in their tent right here on the Belfast Hills. So I stopped short, and found a nook sheltered by weeds below a thorn tree in a Belfast park.

You stop walking, lie down in the bivvybag, and gradually the shaken brain settles and starts to think. What I was lying on must be very close indeed to the line between the Protestant bits of Belfast and the Catholic west. As I was drawing these mental maps, someone started riding a motorbike up and down the path alongside my thorn tree. Or rather, several people did.

Would the next amusement be a semi-automatic weapon, and firing at random into the undergrowth? It didn't seem likely. But it did seem possible. So I was glad when it started to rain. The scramblebikers didn't want to scramblebike in the rain, and bikered off.

It got dark. The rain continued. It dripped through the thorn branches, and I made a sort of tent end to my bivvy by bootlacing it to a twig. A pungent aroma arose from the weedbed around me. Water puddled in the hollows of the bivvybag, flowing off when I moved. And gradually but inescapably the inside of the bag was getting damp.

A short time later it stopped getting damp and started getting wet. My gloved hands were wrinkling, as after long washing-up. The water pattered on the weeds, dripped on the twigs, and made a continuous soft rustle of the surroundings. Even through the sleeping bag I could feel the lumps of water as they came down off the twig-ends and onto me. It was actually quite warm.

At grey dawn I arose, squeezed out my clothes, and immediately got soaked again pushing through the wet weedbed.

FURTHER SUFFERING

Those monks who used to live on the tops of pillars in the desert ruthlessly abstaining from everything – one St Simeon Stylites is actually in the *Guinness Book of Records* for his 45 years up one. Were they just showing off, or were they actually having fun? You really can't tell till you've tried.

There is for some the masochistic pleasure of not having any fun. The author of *Venus in Furs*, Leopold von Sacher-Masoch himself, whenever Wanda was losing her enthusiasm for tying him to the bedpost, used to set off into the Carpathians on a donkey. Eight years later, that other donkeyman Robert Louis Stevenson might just have been copying his ideas. Did Leopold also take a bivvybag? A *fur-lined* bivvybag? The very idea induces a delicious shiver…

People who don't smoke or drink also tend to have sexual intercourse less often. And I suspect, though this has not been studied by sociologists, that they also prefer the Pennines to the Isle of Skye, and the B&B to the bivvybag.

Part – and it's a large part – of the pleasure and satisfaction of climbing rocks is to be confident and safe in a place where, if you weren't so confident and safe, you'd be a trembling wreck and shortly afterwards dead. To have the nut in its crack and know that it's going to stay there; to put the foot on the very small hold and step up with 150m/500ft of air below 95 per cent of the bootsole. Again, to be on hilltops in sleet and low cloud, knowing that the Gore-tex garment and the compass bearings are going to get you down again.

There are those who enjoy the adrenaline experience of being scared in the face of death. A hundred feet up without a runner, the scrabbling on the sloping rock, the lichen flying from the footholds, the last-chance handhold that just has to be there beyond the bulge. Adrenaline is addictive, and the adrenaline life, though short, may well be a happy one. But adventure has been defined as being just on the near side of fear: to be confident and in control in a situation where things could get very nasty, but aren't going to. Such situations do not occur in computer programming or tai-kwon-do.

You don't have to be a theologian to see that in our cushioned world, a little bit of physical discomfort isn't necessarily a bad thing. Dawn is fine from between two boulders at the summit of Kirk Fell; but better far when that new sun is not just brightness to the eye but also the drying out of the sleeping bag after a night of shivering misery. And the day when you park at Pen-y-Pass, walk gently up Glyder Fawr without any blisters, and eat a sandwich in the sun – this is not the day that burns afterwards in the memory.

Accordingly, the following paragraphs on how to diminish that misery are heretical. They should be taken out of the book and burned…

WHAT IF IT RAINS?

'What happens when it rains?' asked the man in the Feshie bothy. The answer is surprisingly simple. What happens is, you get wet.

Rain falls on the outside of the bag; the inside of the bag gets wet; accordingly, it must be leaking. And who wants to walk on across Ulster with a wet sleeper and a leaky bivvy?

The errors were falling thicker than rain on the Emerald Isle. The sleeping bag was not wet. If you get picky about your personal surroundings and decide to wash your sleeping bag you discover that a wet sleeping bag is so heavy it pulls your arms down: it certainly doesn't come dry in half an hour when the sun comes out in Belfast Harbour and you hang it over the ship's rail in the breeze.

And the bivvybag was not leaking. In fact, as I'd treated it with a tent waterproofer, it was not leaking even more seriously than it was designed to not leak.

For moisture to pass across the breathable membrane of the bivvybag it needs to be:

- warmer on the inside than the outside;
- more humid on the inside than the outside;
- have a breeze across the surface.

If none of these is the case, then you might as well be lying inside that impermeable orange plastic. I hadn't been sleeping in Irish rain – but in Scottish condensation. And worse, I'd failed to believe in my bag. Even the tent waterproofer – as we'll see below – had been a roundabout way of getting wetter.

There are basically two sorts of breathable material. A microporous material, such as Gore-tex, has billions of tiny holes. The holes are several thousand times smaller than a water droplet, but still much, much bigger than a molecule of water vapour.

A hydrophilic material, such as Milair, works in a different way. It is completely waterproof, but the long molecules it's made of can pick up a single molecule of water vapour, pass it along the chain, and shrug it off at the other end. The hydrophilic molecule can be simple polyurethane, as in varnish.

Microporous material is made up in three layers – it needs an inner lining to hold in place the Teflon with all the tiny holes in. So, although it is slightly more effective than hydrophilic, it is rather heavier and quite a bit more expensive. To determine whether your bag is microporous, just examine the price ticket.

A breathable membrane can pass water at a rate of 200g per square metre per hour, when the temperature inside it is 30°C, the temperature of the air outside is 21°C, the relative humidity is 60 per cent, and there's an air flow outside of 2m/sec. This figure is for the thicker sort of Sympatex, but other breathables will be only slightly worse or better.

Before the deluge: Slieve Bearnagh in the Mournes

For a person in a breathable jacket, just walking around will produce the 2m/sec of air flow, and Britain's climate will produce the necessary temperature difference. So most of your personal dampness will pass out through the jacket except where you're wearing a rucksack on top.

A person asleep produces less personal moisture (especially if they got into the bag slightly cool rather than all hot and sweaty). The chill of night may offer an even more beneficial temperature difference – though wet nights are also warm nights. However, in order to keep warm, that sleeping person has chosen a sheltered corner with as little flowing air as possible. And a sleeping person isn't nearly as efficient at shaking standing water off the outside surface of the membrane.

One remedy, then, is to move higher up the mountain, for a better temperature gradient across the membrane, and use a thinner sleeping bag for the same reason. And for air flow, sleep out on a small knoll. As you fall asleep you'll be pleasantly dry all over – and an hour later you'll wake up shivering. For this is the basic law of the bivvy:

THE WARMER THE WETTER.

Or to put it more bluntly:

SHIVER – OR DRIP.

LOOK AFTER YOUR BIVVY
AND YOUR BIVVY WILL LOOK AFTER YOU

A bivvy really is not at all a tent. A tent is a thing. You pitch it at nightfall, and if the rain comes in you complain to the shop and get your money back.

A bivvybag, we recall, is not so much a thing as a surly Asturian person called Miguel. If Miguel approves of you he'll take you to some wonderful places. If your behaviour is inappropriate – you've made some remark about Mont Blanc or Snowdon, you've been rude about the food – he'll desert you in the middle of nowhere and let you cope on your own. Or worse, he'll walk just a little too fast, and take you somewhere where, if you weren't such an over-civilised wimp, you'd really enjoy, and laugh behind his tangly beard.

It's important, then, to retain the respect of your bag. We none of us like to be sniggered at by our equipment…

- Like a tent, it must not be stored wet. Unlike a tent, it's pretty quick and easy to dry. Ten minutes in a brisk wind will do it.
- The people who make the bivvybag say it should be hung up in a wardrobe. The people who made your sleeping bag want you to hang that in your wardrobe as well. Even without the rainbow

selection of high-performance outdoor outerwear that I don't possess, my wardrobe is full of my clothes. The manufacturers grumble, but give in: the bag won't come to much harm provided I don't stuff it in the stuff bag. Roll it up gently from the toe, bend it in two or in three, and slide the stuff bag over it.

- Don't lay it on scree or sharp stones. You wouldn't want to anyway, but if on the summit of Ben More Mull, say, and with a foam mat, put the foam mat underneath the bivvybag. (On soft grass, on the other hand, it's better to have the foam inside the bag – this keeps it from sliding away in the night.)

- Keep it clean, as dirt blocks its microscopic holes and smothers it. Wash the bag gently in soap flakes by hand. Do not use detergents, as these interfere with the mystic chemistry of the hydrophilics. They also sabotage the expensive coating you're about to spray on. If you're really fond of your bag, give it Nikwax Loft Techwash – this removes detergent residues from when you washed it wrongly the last time.

- Don't waterproof the bag with waterproofing as this too will smother the pores. If you believe the bag is leaking, I've just carefully explained that it isn't. The time when it needs reproofing is when it is wetting out: moisture is penetrating into the material, making it heavy when wet and difficult to dry. Re-coat it with a product such as Nikwax TX Direct spray, or with Granger's Superpruf – these are specifically designed for breathable fabrics. Older products coat the fabric with silicon, which is fairly cheap but doesn't last very long. Superpruf is a fluorocarbon, which is a lot more expensive. Either way, the effect should be to make water falling onto the fabric roll into droplets and fall off.

- After washing, and after applying any coating, gentle heat treatment is supposed to improve the 'roll into droplets and fall off' effect. Julian Miles suggests for his Milair bag that you iron it from the outside with a very cool iron (well below the nylon setting) to revitalise the coating. A different manufacturer suggests 'steam iron warm' for their Gore-tex bag. But only if you really think it needs revitalising: there's a risk of sticking together the front and back if it accidentally folds under the iron. A warm but not hot tumble-drying has also been suggested.

The best source of information is the swing ticket that dangled from the bag when you bought it. But as you've lost the ticket, you'll have to switch on your search engine and find the bagmaker's website, or those of Nikwax and Granger (currently Nikwax.com and Granger.co.uk). The instructions above are for when your bag's so ancient you can't remember who made the bag and the label's rubbed off. They may also reassure you that when you find a care label with an ironing temperature, this isn't as silly as it seems.

• If the taped seams have broken down, a phone call to the manufacturer will reveal that it could be repaired but will cost so much you might as well replace the whole bag. In which case, you risk little by attempting to apply cloth-backed tape (hot melt tape) with a hot iron. Pennine Outdoor is one supplier for this. Use the tip of the iron until the hot glue bubbles out, being careful not to scorch the bag fabric.

• Less excitingly, you can try applying waterproof (rather than breathable) sealant to the outside of the leaky seam. Granger's Sports Glue would do. Do this before applying any coating to the bag as a whole, as it won't stick if you do it after.

• If the bivvybag has been stored wet it will start to degrade: first it will wet out, but after that its inner coating may start to blister or peel away. Get a new bag and this time store it dry…

Midges

All worthwhile tents are screened and netted against the evil insect. Some bivvybags are too. But if there are midges then it must be summer – so shouldn't you be further up the hill?

Midges rarely annoy above the 600m/2000ft contour. In a zipless bag in a damp wood at the foot of Ben Nevis, I made a strange discovery. When I scrunched everything up to leave a very small breathing hole, the midges did not come in. Perhaps the air was moving in and out rapidly enough to scare them off.

Which leads to the next technicality:

How big a hole?

In a tent you simply go to sleep. In a bag, you're constantly interacting with the surroundings in an interesting way. Would you like to be slightly warmer than you are? Or would you prefer to be slightly drier? To a certain extent this can be controlled by the size of the breathing aperture.

In a well-maintained bag, it is possible to zip yourself right up inside it and still breathe. From the outside you now resemble a large green slug, but if you care about appearances you are perhaps not a bivvybag person in the first place. Some find it unpleasantly stuffy. More seriously, however, whilst you are retaining all the warmth of your breathed-out air, you're also retaining all its moisture.

Zipping in completely makes you a bit warmer, but quite a lot damper. It's good to do the zip right up during a vicious squall while the wind and rain gust from all directions, and you're waiting for it to ease up a bit before opening a small hole and groping in the rucksack for a pork pie and an old sandwich. Total closure gives a slight but pleasant sensation of shelter and security.

But as soon as the squall's passed over, it's better to keep open a small hole to breathe through. Enjoy fresh air, and avoid challenging the micropores or the polyurethane with the extra dampness from the lungs. You can arrange a sort of chamber so that outgoing breath mixes with and warms the incoming fresh air. And at the start of the night, when it's still relatively warm, it's best to have the head right out and enjoy the sunset.

One authority suggests that, zipped right into a hydrophilic-type bag, it's possible to suffocate to death. Even, perhaps, in a microporous one if it's really dirty. But I don't believe this. Certainly it's never happened to me so far.

THE IDEAL SITE

Continuous interaction with the surroundings – walking over it but also absorbing and being absorbed, giving and taking in return – is the point of being outdoors. And so, half an hour before dark, you start to eye up the boulders, lie down and get up again, feel the wind and assess the quality of the light. Do I want to be romantic, or do I want to be comfortable? This dip is out of the wind, but am I prepared to sacrifice the streetlights as they come on across the Vale of York?

The six requirements of a bivvyplace are below. It's impossible to have all six on the same night as some of them contradict each other. This is why you need to spend lots and lots of nights in your bag.

1 The view

Hilltop or clifftop is best – except if the hilltop's a flat plateau, when it's better to be a little way down the side. But the sunset side, or the one facing the sunrise? Either way, you want a lake for the reflections.

2 Shelter

Wind comes suddenly in the night. The bag isn't going to blow down, of course, but when wind moulds it against the body it gets very cold. So it's good to have a hollow below a rock or a clump of trees close enough to roll into.

3 Warmth

The clear starry nights are the really cold ones. Anything at all between the sleeper and the night sky helps here – even the leafless twigs of a thorn.

4 Softness

Dry dead grasses and heather – they don't just add to the comfort but also to the warmth, as most heat is lost into the ground. Really tufty heather is luxury enough to sacrifice even a hilltop view for.

Ground can deceive. Really soft-looking moss can have rocks under. Lie on the ground before deciding to make a bed of it. Once you've changed into the dry socks it's a bit late to discover you should be lying in a larchwood rather than poplar. (Twisty roots and lack of leafmould is why poplar should really be renamed as 'un-poplar'.)

Backpacking rucksacks are well padded, and an empty one makes a partial mattress. This means taking a large plastic bag or sack-liner for all the stuff that would otherwise be in the rucksack.

5 Flatness

You're not pegged down, and bag fabric is slippery. So if there's a slope you may well end up at the bottom.

6 Privacy

'Those who go to sleep in a field', says the Chinese proverb, 'will be found in a field, asleep.' But nobody notices a bivvybag.

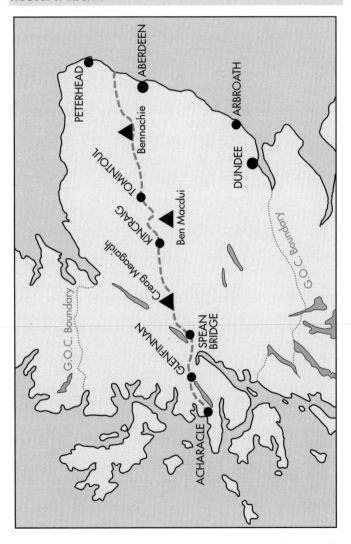

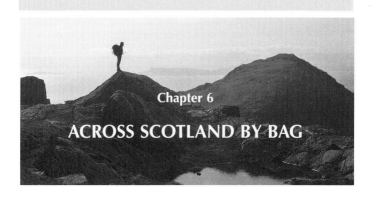

Chapter 6

ACROSS SCOTLAND BY BAG

'Better a thousand times that he should be a tramp, and mend pots and pans by the wayside, and sleep under the trees, and see the dawn and the sunset every day above a new horizon.'

Robert Louis Stevenson

WETNESS AND WEIGHT: Cross-Scotland constraints

And yet, with all the excitement of being out there in the environment and the weather – the moral benefits of a bit of misery – the second night in a wet bivvy can get depressing, and also rather smelly. So for a serious crossing of Scotland I like to have some sort of roof somewhere that I could get to if necessary. This means a bothy or better. And if tonight doesn't have a roof, then tomorrow night must have not just a roof but a drying room: a youth hostel, say, or a five-star hotel. (I expect five-star hotels have drying rooms.)

And there's no point in carrying a light pack if it's full of heavy food. Rough calculations suggest that it's worth walking an extra mile to avoid carrying a day's food (1kg/2lb) for one extra day. Take a hill stint of six days: if you walked out to a shop at the end of the second day, that would save carrying an extra four days' food for each of the first two days. Thus it's worth an eight-mile detour to get to the shop.

A simpler rule, for Scotland anyway, is that more than three days' food is too much.

- For every bivvy night, **either** an available roof (bothy or better) – this may involve a diversion into a nearby valley
- **or** on the following night a roof plus dry-out (possibly involving diversion).
- For every high-level day, a FWA (foul weather alternative) low-level route of good quality (paths and passes, not roads).
- At least twice: a long stint (two days minimum) through roadless country.
- Ten Munros close enough to include; plus some Corbetts.
- One really nice inn along the way.

ACHARACLE TO ABERDEENSHIRE

The best-laid plans of mice and men... and there's something definitely mouselike about the man in the bag huddled down among the stalks of grass. In 1999 the whole bivvybag cross-Scotland scheme fell to pieces. High pressure settled over the UK, it was far too hot to sleep anywhere below 600m/2000ft, and the route-plan floated away like a buzzard and vanished into the blue. Five days later, when it started to rain, I had to wonder where I was meant to be...

On Druim Fiaclach, looking around for the ideal bag-site

The Moidart Corbetts have grassy ridges, steep stony sides, and lots and lots of lochs to look at. The rucksacks were fairly heavy – mine had four days' food – so we hauled them a little bit at a time over Rois-bheinn, dropped them for an outing to An Stac, and wandered on over Sgurr na Ba Glaise. The air was warm and windless, the sea glittered under the afternoon sun. It was still only six o'clock, but Colin wanted to turn back to his car next day and be up slating roofs on Monday. So Druim Fiaclach had to be it for the day.

When there's time to kill at day's end in May, Druim Fiaclach is the place to kill it. There are grassy corners, little rock-walls and little pools. We found the ideal grassy corner for the bivvy, sheltered by one of the little rock-walls, a little pool nearby. But the rock-wall did interrupt some of the sea view – so we spent half an hour finding an even better one. And then another half an hour scrambling over the rock-walls and looking at the lochs. Then we did it all again, this time taking photos. And then it was time for tea.

Colin, turning back tomorrow, doesn't mind luggage. And it's a warm evening. So we have hot food, sitting on our grassy ledge, with our feet dangling into the deep hollow of Glen Aladale.

This is Colin's first attempt at true outdoor living. He can't believe that you just lie down on the ground, stare up at the sky till you're tired of it, then shut your eyes. Meanwhile I'm still up taking pictures of the sunset. This far north, at this time of year, sunset lasts for about two hours. The sea is striped by islands into bands of different sorts of orange. Long silvery lochs divide the black land. White fluffy clouds form out of nowhere, rush briefly towards us and then dissolve. Like the waves of a rising tide, the next band of cloud comes further up, then the sunset comes back, and finally a wave of white surges through the gaps of the ridge and breaks over our heads. Colin, happening to open one eye, is surprised to see no stars or dark mountain outlines. 'Hey – what's happened to my view?' he wants to know.

On the second day I pushed on alone over clouded Corbetts. Glenfinnan – with its tempting sleeping-car bunkhouse – was to be the first drying-out point. But I was still dry, and so was the weather, so it was on to more mountains. At six the cloud broke, at half-past six the sun came out, and at seven I was on top of Sgurr nan Coireachan.

Bonnie Prince Charlie spent a night up here in 1746 (damp, midge-bitten, but consoled with whisky). Most Munro-baggers since have simply touched the cairn and away. But the Bonnie Prince had the right of it.

Coireachan is even better than Moidart was. There's a grassy nook right beside the cairn, so if I should get bored of the Rum view westward I need only sit up in bed to receive the Glendessarry view to the east.

Not that the Rum view is at all boring. The sunset this time is delicately tinted in pink and grey. As well as Rum there are the Outer Hebrides drifting along the horizon like spaced-out whales, and on the right, the multicoloured sky runs down to black Skye.

Sunset moves gradually round into the north and becomes sunrise. A chilly little breeze is flicking around the summit cairn and down into my hollow. The new day's weather is cruel. I only want to leap out, roll up the bag and warm up with a brisk stride down the ridge. But that cold air is also crystal clear, with Ben Wyvis poking up in the far northeast behind all the main mountains of Glen Affric. Which means careful work with exposures and tripod, and then leap up and down a little to stop shivering and press the shutter button.

Photography is a matter not just of the best equipment, but also of creativity and an eye, and not making a mess of the exposure. On the other hand, you can get quite a long way simply by being high at the right time of day… The fluffy clouds are back, but not in the sky: they fill the valleys, surge over the passes, and make my morning ridge into a series of pointed islands. Low sun and clouds underfoot: it's so obvious there's going to be a Brocken Spectre that when it suddenly arrives I've got the camera out ready to take its picture.

Until they develop a digital reference library small and waterproof enough for the rucksack, the wonderings one wonders across the ridges of Scotland will remain unresolved, mostly. I was doing this walk within the Great Outdoor Challenge, which is a slightly organised way for 250 people to walk across Scotland by many routes in the same two weeks in May. Is there any Munro in the Challenge area that hasn't been crossed on the Challenge? Perhaps Ben Lomond – briefly in the late eighties within the southern boundary – but perhaps again not. Which is the most frequently Challenge-bagged Munro? Mount Keen, easy.

But somewhere, lurking among the statistics, there may be one or two un-Challenge-bagged Corbetts. Beinn Bheula, by that wandering southern boundary. Beinn Bhan of Applecross. Perhaps even Beinn Bhan above Gairlochy, I thought, as I wandered towards it in warm but fading evening light.

Well, I was the only one this year, that's for sure. And in the boggy bit after Meall a' Phubuill I entertained myself by composing a money-back demand to Challenge Control. This GOC is supposed to be a social event, and I hadn't met a soul since Acharacle, still less any of the Challenged.

With the approach of bedtime it got colder, and clearer. Low sun from the north fell on Ben Nevis and briefly warmed the fingers of any late climbers before their short benightment. Loch Linnhe glittered, and the stony plateau of Beinn Bhan was, at only 800m/2600ft, the top of the world. I trotted down to the first cosy peat hag and unrolled the bag. Spean Bridge with its hordes tomorrow; but for tonight, at least, a bedroom to myself.

The overnight view had no sea in it, and only a single loch. Apart from Ben Nevis the hills below the sunset were rounded ones of Central Scotland. This was not a night of wild horizons. This was a night of comfort.

The ideal site combines soft grass, a windbreak and a view

Wind whispered in the grass, but didn't get down into my peat hag. Dry peat was softer than any manmade mattress and smelt nice as well. I was warm enough to leave my face out in the fresh night air all night long. I almost overslept – but sun shining straight into the eyes is better than any alarm clock. At seven I set off downhill. In three minutes I saw a strange yellow shape. Something to do with sheep? No. It was, of course, Challenger Number 17, Han Bakker of Holland, smiling from his tent and offering cups of tea.

I learnt my lesson. Carn na Fhreiceadain is a Corbett that's nowhere in particular rather to the east of the Monadh Liath. Was it Challenger-free? Was it Fhreiceadain. That one had Number 247, Jonathan Worters of Scarborough, in from Torridon over Loch Ness. 'Is that Northern Monadhliath better than it looks on the map, then?' 'No,' says Mr Worters: 'it's worse.'

On the Challenge, it's almost eccentric not to be an eccentric Corbett-bagger. And probably, after a long trawl through the route-plans, you'd find none within the boundaries unscaled.

The hills of the west are steep; the Cairngorms are rounded, but big; elsewhere, in the east, the hills are merely rounded. Section Nine of Munro's Tables is, some would argue, the least thrilling section of them all. (Others fiercely contend that Section Five, the A9 Hills around Drumochter, is a lot less interesting even than Section Nine.)

When the hills won't co-operate, you just have to make your own fun. Walking has something to do with feet, certainly, but mostly it takes place in the mind. Thus, above Glen Roy, one climbs up the rough grasses of Carn Dearg; and then one climbs up the rough grasses of Carn Dearg; and then one climbs up the rough grasses of Carn Dearg. Carn Dearg means 'reddish heap of stones', and three hills – all of them Corbetts – carry this distinctive name. Was this just a muddled mapmaker (one reddish pile being much like any other)? Or is it more sinister, a cover-up: the denizens of Section Nine trying to pretend that it has fewer dull hills than it does?

The civilised amenities of Spean Bridge, slight though they be, had unstiffened my high resolve. I stopped short of the stony reddish tops and slept in deep heather beside a stream, almost too low on the hill for a proper view even. It didn't matter. Tramping that deep heather with a sack full of food meant that this fourth night was one for simple sleep. At dawn, haze and horizontal sunbeams turned the rounded lumps into a succession of pastel blues, fading and receding. The soft-focus composition needed a sharp accent somewhere; so an obliging eagle rose from among the Carn Deargs at my feet.

There are five Munros around Creag Meagaidh: five in a long line between Loch Ness and the A86. At noon I stood on the western one. There followed seven hours of gentle grassy slopes and gravel plateau. Creag Meagaidh itself is not all that boring – its plateau is amoeboid, a thing of many blobs. You walk a lawnlike curve and suddenly there's a drop of crag and old snow and a huge corrie with a lochan in it. The corries come at you from all directions, and it's a tricky place in a blizzard.

The long ridge of Carn Liath (grey pile of stones) runs eastwards into the evening. These smooth hills have no rock hollows, but a little dip and a rucksack to windward provide just enough shelter. The chill breeze passing a few inches overhead means there's none of the stuffiness associated with zipped-in tent living. Moonlight shivers across Loch Laggan. On a nearby ridge at midnight, a stag stands against the silvery background.

The sixth dawn was a grey one, and with rain on the way. My boots were wet from snowfields of the previous day, and I felt I was displaying real strength of character as I rolled away the dry nightsocks and got back into the damp footwear of the new day.

The Monadhliath Munros comprise a Carn Ban (white pile of stones), a Carn Dearg (red stones, remember?) and a Geal Charn (pile of stones of off-white colour). Walk them as fast as you can, driven on by the odd sharp shower; descend over an afternoon's worth of deep heather on defeated feet; and really appreciate the barmeal and bunkhouse at Kincraig. There's a shop there as well.

I looked out of the Kirkbeag bunkhouse at the wind whipping the birch branches, and the clouds above them intent on breaking every Great Outdoor Challenge rule by running across Scotland coast-to-coast in under three hours. It didn't seem to be a day for the Braeriach Plateau, it really didn't. Being part of a great project like the GOC carries rewards, but also responsibilities: it would be disgraceful to spoil the event's no-fatalities-so-far record simply for the sake of mopping up four Munros.

So I opened up my map and looked south. That seemed like a very long way, and besides, everybody goes up Glen Feshie. So then I looked north, and there was the Rothiemurchus Forest.

After a few nasty experiences involving twigs and ditches we learn to avoid the map's green patches with the little Christmas-tree markings. Rothiemurchus, though, is not a wood-pulp factory. It hasn't been grown simply to be torn down and made into – let's say – the next 100,000 copies of *A Walk in the Woods*. Hillwriters tend to think rather frequently of Bill Bryson's book, about a long-distance walk that he didn't even complete, that somehow managed to slip out of its boots and hop from the category 'Outdoors' across to the category 'Bestsellers'. Well, the bit about getting torn to pieces by bears is genuinely amusing. But I can't help wishing I could invite Bill Bryson along with me through the Rothiemurchus forest.

The Appalachian Trail has 370 sorts of tree – Americans do tend to overdo things – while Rothiemurchus has just three. But how many different things Rothiemurchus can do with Scots pine, birch and juniper. There are the thickets where the pines stand close and dark and straight, with the occasional white birch trunk as surprising as a nude in a nunnery. There's the recolonised scrub, where the three trees grow so close that you can see only a few yards of sandy path in front, and the high heather cone of Lurcher's Crag overhead. And there is the clearing, floored with grass and bright bilberry, where pines are old and twisty above the little wooden bothy of Scottish Natural Heritage.

For this is managed land, carefully crafted into a synthetic wilderness that never was, haunted by beavers but also by backpackers, by mountain hares and mountainbikers, by the pine marten and the person with sandwich and plastic mac. Wilderness is all very well, but give me the sandy, stony path and the Cairngorm Club footbridge on a nasty day when the wind lashes the treetops and makes white waves on the lochans.

The Appalachian Trail is 2500 miles long (Americans really do overdo things); the paths through Rothiemurchus are just 15 miles, and then it's time for something else. The track leads out past the Reindeer Centre and through the narrow pass of Ryvoan into the bare hills. Here are granite boulders, and heather, and a lot of wind. Sun patches and sharp squalls chase each other across the brown slopes, and down the

South Cluanie Ridge at evening on a bivvybag trip in April

Top of Garbh-bheinn at nightfall, with Loch Sunart

Sleepy Hollow: dawn over Ullswater from Sheffield Pike

Snowy bivvy on Ben Ledi *(photo by Colin Brash)*

On Gulvain, looking back to Moidart (Chapter 6)

Best in the wet: walking in Rothiemurchus Forest

hill comes a hillwalker. The wind picked him up off Bynack More and hurled him against a boulder, and he's pretty sure he's cracked a rib.

The bad weather has already done me some good in terms of Munro-count: four not ticked off on the Braeriach Plateau will be a real help when it comes to still having some good ones to do in my seventies. Now, though, it can confer a Corbett benefit. For when, to defer the evil day of Munro Completion, one turns to the Corbetts, how sad to find the 50 real goodies already done (Merrick and Morrone, Goatfell and the Cobbler and Beinn Dearg of Torridon) and only the dun humps of the east to console one's declining years. Invest, then, in the future; and do a dun hump today.

Except that it didn't quite work like that.

Every Corbett must drop at least 152m/500ft to some defining col. But it's almost naughty to be crossing that defining col anyway – it leads to Fords of Avon – and to snatch a whole Corbett with only 165m/540ft of added climb is as pleasing as stealing sweeties. But pleasure of a more solid sort was at the top of the 165 metres. The summit of Creag Mhor is proper Cairngorm plateau, with pink gravel and granite. Most of the full-size Cairngorms have flat tops, but here one of the granite hummocks is the actual summit.

I stood on the rough granite, leaning into a wind that was just not strong enough to be scary, with one of the bursts of sunlight sparkling on the crystals of the rock. Cloud streaked and striped across the blue, and swirled in the hollow of Loch Avon. Between the clouds the sun was low and turning yellow. And it was one of those mountain moments when you thank God – or geology – for making Scotland the way it is, and the size it is. How right it feels to be a human being, in a decent breathable jacket, in Rothiemurchus in a gale and on the hummock of Creag Mhor at sunset. Just to put the icing on the cake, on the way down to Fords of Avon it started to snow.

Sometimes the bad weather days can be the best days of all.

The night when it snows on your bivvybag isn't one that you enjoy at the time. Somehow it doesn't feel right to have a clammy wet weight lying on top of you, so you knock it off, and then when you roll over the clammy wet is all underneath. Then in the morning there is the wet breakfast eaten in wet gloves; the boots with snow inside; the semi-frozen water bottle. Nasty to live through, these nights are the ones you look back on with vivid memory and affection – the surprising white surroundings, the snowflakes in the eyebrows, the rapid warming induced by the day's first steps through the slush-covered heather...

On the other hand, there's the metal box left by the Fleet Air Arm at Fords of Avon. When it comes to choosing between memories later and a metal box tonight, the metal box has it every time. Decomposing heather makes a soft if soggy bed, and the place warms up even further when two more of the Challenged arrive with a bottle of whisky.

The weather stayed unpleasant, so I stayed at the bunkhouse that leans against a rather grand hotel in Tomintoul. The following night, deep heather on a grouse-shooters' hill in unknown Aberdeenshire offered an even more comfortable resting-place. And the night after that I lay among the sand dunes and watched the sun rise out of the North Sea. I lay late to let the bag dry, then wandered back inland looking for a cafe with proper coffee and a railway train heading south.

Fords of Avon shelter under May snowfall

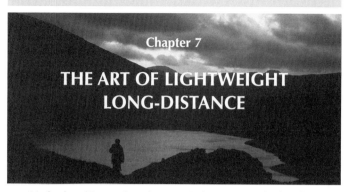

Chapter 7

THE ART OF LIGHTWEIGHT LONG-DISTANCE

'My husband is a real outdoor survival expert. For the last three months he has lived in a den on the riverbank, and eaten nothing but fish which he catches himself by diving underwater.

Mind you, he is an otter.'

Mrs Otter, River Exe, Devon
(letter to *Viz* magazine 1995)

There are five rules for covering country:

1 Travel light

A sack below 14kg/30lb is the one luxury that matters.

2 Start early

Why waste batteries at night, then spend good morning daylight lying in bed? Shift to Central European time: get up at dawn and fall asleep at what we call 8pm but the Ukrainians call bedtime.

3 Start slowly

When I set out over all the hills of Southern Scotland, I was chasing a record of Colin Donnelly. Donnelly is one of the fastest hill men in Scotland and roughly twice as fast as me. Each day he ran – very fast – from 9am till 5pm. Each day I ran – rather slowly – from 5am till 9pm; and I ended up two days ahead.

You don't go far by going fast. Going fast just gets you tired. You go far by going for a long time.

4 Finish late

Which also solves the problem of how to pass the evening in the confines of the bivvybag. Don't get into the bivvy till the evening's already over.

5 Eat, drink and be considerably less miserable

Travelling a long distance fairly quickly is as much a matter of eating as of the feet. The section below suggests 1kg/2lb of food a day, which is rather a lot. Don't wait till you feel hungry. Tell yourself that if you don't eat this food you'll have to carry it even further. Have muesli and Mars bars in the pockets to nibble as you go along. Slow down, and put more effort into the eating.

Slimmers pinch flesh at the side of the waist to see how fat they are. This also works in reverse. About 2cm of pinchable body is a healthy minimum. When, after five days, you find nothing between skin and ribs, you're about to flake out. You may have walked far and fast but you've failed at the eating, and the rest of the journey is going to be less fun-filled.

BAG AND BAGGAGE

This section appears to be about being mean and stingy. In fact, it's about practicalities. If there was a £90 emergency layer that wrapped up smaller and weighed less than a binliner with three holes cut out, then of course I would be telling you to spend that £90. However, there isn't: and the choice is simply between the binliner in damp-ashes grey or classic black.

It's an odd fact that as equipment gets lighter and lighter, the weight of the rucksack stays the same. The Roman legionary carried the same load on his back as the Para in the Falklands in 1984 – that load of 35kg/80lb being the most a man can actually carry and still function in mud. It takes a real creative effort to take things out of the rucksack and leave them behind.

A pair of dry socks for the morning? You'll enjoy them for about 10 minutes, which is how long it'll take them to get as wet as the others. But you'll enjoy not carrying the extra 8oz of weight all the way across Scotland.

Our legs and shoulders vary as much as our personalities. For me there are two rucksack thresholds. Below about 10kg/20lb the rucksack doesn't really matter. Whereas above about 15kg/35lb it matters every step of the way. Nothing (except food) justifies taking the sack above the upper threshold. Rigorous deniers of the flesh – such as hillrunners – can take a three-day walk while staying below the 10kg. This means that the walking holiday will be stripped of any pleasure it might have contained, apart from one: that of walking, unburdened, from dawn to dark through the wilderness.

One of my local shopkeepers told me he was going to take up hillwalking for the sake of his heart. Excellent idea: not just good for the heart, good for the soul as well (though somewhat damaging to the soles of the feet).

I was in again a month later. And he was very pleased: he'd made a start. He'd been down to Ambleside and spent £300. The jacket was a fairly cheap mid-price sort of one, so I said yes, even the fairly cheap mid-price ones are good enough for the Himalaya up to about 6000m/20,000ft. The boots – those made by Mr Brasher – are perfectly good. And then the gaiters. I always get embarrassed about the gaiters. Gaiters are very useful and necessary items, ornamental too in a heavy-legged sort of way. It's just that I've never had occasion to own a pair.

There's a definite pleasure in having equipment that looks good and is good: that really does keep the rain out, or the heat in, your feet on the rockface or the correct trail. And if it doesn't, you can take it back to the shop and they'll hide it behind the counter and give you a new one.

There's a contrary pleasure: in having stuff that looks as if you've been out on the mountains for a long, long time; stuff that, if it gets annoying, you can stuff in a litter bin. This is the bottom gear: if you lose it you don't mind because the replacement is going to be better; it doesn't matter if it gets dirty; it actually can't get dirty because it already is.

This section is about that contrary pleasure. It's about the charms of dispossession, about having a lovely light rucksack during the day and an austere and funless evening.

Many walking handbooks list the things to take. Here is a list of things to leave behind.

Spare clothes

Suppose all of your clothes were wet and all of them on. If that's enough to let you survive the storm, then that's the clothes you actually can't do without – three wet layers and a waterproof.

No dry clothes for next day? Well, if it's raining next day then those dry clothes would very soon be wet ones. And if it isn't raining, then these wet clothes will very soon be dry.

Waterproofs

A substantial breathable jacket in cheerful crimson or purple, with armpit zips, useful pockets, taped seams and all, weighs about 1.1kg/2lb – and when it isn't raining, all that weight is in your rucksack. Worse, when it has been raining, all that weight is in your rucksack wet.

But wear a single-skin waterproof (which always comes in green for some reason) and a fleece underneath – when it isn't raining the waterproof (500g/1lb 2oz) stuffs away in the lid rather than half the sack, and the fleece is still on and drying in the breeze.

And then in bed you can keep the fleece while dispensing with the damp crackle of the waterproof.

Sleeping bag

Down or feather bags are light and very warm – until they get wet. Bivvybagging involves condensation at best, and getting into bed in wet clothes at worst – so I take a lightweight synthetic sleeping bag.

As with the clothes, there should be sleeping bag enough to keep warm at night when it's completely wet and you're wearing all your clothes inside it and they're completely wet as well. It makes more sense to carry 8oz of clothes, which can be worn day or night, than 8oz of extra bag.

Thus we arrive at the one-season synthetic bag. Ones designed for mountain marathons are tight-fitting, not terribly sturdy in construction, cost from £60 and weigh 1kg/2lb 4oz.

Sleeping mat

A mat is not simply for softies to protect their poor bones from the hard ground. In terms of warmth for weight, a mat is quite a useful item.

Unless it's very windy, you lose more heat into the ground than into the sky. Also, the sleeping bag underneath you is squashed, so it's less effective. Instead of a warm thick sleeping bag, I'd carry the same weight as a thin bag plus mat.

On the other hand, the rolled mat goes inside the sack – in which case you need a bigger and heavier sack – or else it gets tied on the outside, where it catches the wind, and everyone who passes can see you're some sort of long-distance sleeper.

The closed-cell foam mat weighs about 250g/9oz and costs £10. There is also the inflatable sort, more expensive (£50), weighs about 350g/12oz, with Therma-rest being the main brandname. The extra 3oz is more than countered by being able to use a smaller sack. The Therma-rest is tough, puncturing only when used as a bobsleigh by eight-year-old nieces. It can be repaired with a bicycle puncture kit.

And there is also no mat at all. Walk far enough during the day, and you won't need comfort at night. If you take the time to find deep dead grass or heather, that will insulate as well as closed-cell foam. For nights on the wooden shelves of bothies, however, some mat is essential between the bones and the timber. You can't always count on finding a sheet of bubblewrap along the shoreline at Sourlies.

Actually, bubblewrap is excellent, especially the sort with really big bubbles. But if you roll over, your bed may blow away on the breeze – so put the bubblewrap inside the bivvy. In caves or on stony surfaces, it's better to have the bedmat or bubblewrap outside, to protect the bivvybag from scratches.

There's more good padding in your rucksack. Empty its contents into a big plastic bag and put it under the bivvybag as a mattress at hip or shoulder level.

Boots

A hundred grams on the feet has the same effect as 500g on the back. Therefore, the boots should be the lightest the walker feels comfortable and safe in. If the walker is a runner the boots will, accordingly, be shoes. Runners regard ankles as their most important organs: they train themselves to fall painfully onto the stones rather than put weight on a wrongly placed foot.

On the principle of 'buy the second-cheapest', I once experimented to see just how inexpensive a boot could be and still get me across Scotland. I worked my way down to a pair at £19.99 from the Sunday market. These really did absorb rather a lot of water when wet, and the treads weren't deep enough for downhill grass. So you probably do need to spend more than £19.99. Lately I've got fed up with the way fabric boots come apart after a single season and am trying the lightest kind of leather ones. But the right boots are the ones that don't give the person inside them a blister.

Cooker, saucepans and fuel

You could eat the same boring dehydrated savoury rice night after night. On the other hand, you could enjoy something really nasty tonight – a meal of dried-milk muesli, pork pies and custard cream biscuits – and a delicious barmeal tomorrow. Cooking in a bivvybag cools you down more than the hot food ever warms you up. Snuggle down inside the zip with those biscuits…

Book for evening reading

Leave the book and just walk further. Walking keeps you warm.

COMPARATIVE LUXURY

Having gone through the list, hard-heartedly leaving behind anything that was there merely to add enjoyment to a long trip across Scotland, you've lightened the sack by at least 3kg/7lb. Which should allow a couple of little luxuries to go back in.

Dry socks at night-time

These allow the feet to turn back from flabby fishes into things reasonably feetlike. This helps prevent blisters, or at least unwrinkles the skin enough for the sticking-plasters to stick to it.

Plastic bags

Placed between dry socks and wet boots, those socks remain dry and can be worn in the evening as well as in bed. More plastic bags let belongings stay out in the cold rather than in the rucksack (as the rucksack is busy being a mattress) or in the bivvy (where Robert Louis Stevenson found 'Desert Pastors' such an awkward bedfellow).

Bothies often have firewood, so a little packet of dry newspaper and matches lights the fire, and the newspaper, if sufficiently racy, provides bedtime reading as well.

And wouldn't it be nice to have some scanty garment to wear in the bar, rather than the wet thermals you just washed?

Even no-nonsense types in the Special Forces have found that a light tarp or basha, stretched above the head end of the bivvy, allows everything to stay quite a bit drier while still not really resembling a tent. A basha (basically a rectangular cloth 2.5 x 1.5m/8 x 5ft with holes at the corners) weighs 250g/9oz, with an extra 160g/6oz for pole and pegs.

Old men should be explorers, says Tennyson. They should also be cunning and comfort-loving; and most important of all, rich. When I get old and rich I shan't be upgrading my bivvybag to make it heavier, but I shall be thinking about a cosy down sleeping bag after all. Cunning means knowing where water might trickle through the zips; breathing out into the open air; locating off-route dryout spots. A down bag can be made to repel dampness with a wash-in proofing – Nikwax do one. But washing feathers is a tricky business, and you can have it done professionally. And a really warm down bag weighs no more than 1.8kg/4lb.

Dry socks, little cooker, tarp cover; in no time at all, those 5kg are back in the sack…

THE FUEL ON THE HILL

Hill life is life at the limits. So it's only appropriate that hill food should be food taken as far as it'll go – and sometimes quite a bit further than that.

Take a humble sachet of cup-a-soup (Golden Chicken flavour), but serve it at the Shelter Stone. The Shelter Stone is a boulder weighing 3000 tons or so, 20 miles from anywhere in the middle of the Cairngorms. Drink the Golden Chicken soaking wet and shivering under some unexpected June snowfall. When I tried this myself, I was unable to believe that so much pleasure could be had for a cost of just nine pence.

Two days earlier we'd walked into Ballater along the old railway, planning our campaign against Ballater's shops. Me to the chemist, because that might shut and we needed sticking plasters more than anything. My companion David to the supermarket with a list – for we meant to get to the youth hostel, get fed, get slightly washed and get, most importantly, into bed. Planned supper for next Sunday night at the Shelter Stone: rice, dehydrated curry, Mars bars.

Two days passed and we reached the Shelter Stone in a shower of snow. Soup supped, still shivering, stove a blue homely glow under the big boulder – David holds out what looks like a lichened lump of Cairngorm granite. David has purchased no dehydrated curry. He has got us a haggis.

It makes sense. The supermarkets of Ballater are like any other supermarkets, only less so. But the butchers of Ballater are the best in the world. A food section needs a recipe in it: here is the recipe for Haggis Shelter Stone.

Per person:
- *400g/1lb haggis*
- *200g/8oz dried mashed potato*
- *butter*

Boil the haggis gently (over a nearly empty gas cylinder, perhaps) for 30 minutes. Lift the haggis out and stir the dried mash into the cooking water. Add butter for extra calories.

None of the high-calorie grease that floats out of the haggis is lost. And if you eat the grease then you don't have to wash it up. When washing-up is with a heather twig in a freezing stream, in the snow, in the dark, anything that makes it easier is appreciated.

This is eating at the extremes – but which extreme? My wife, who wouldn't ever eat anything at all under a 3000 ton boulder, considers that a bad food story. She's wrong. Here is a bad food story.

Because of the bar meals, I never carry cookers in Lakeland. The campsite shop at Langdale has long hours, friendly service – but fairly limited stock. Coffee, perhaps – made up with hot water from the tap? Ingenious, but there will be no hot tap at Angle Tarn. What we ended up with, at six the next morning, was little packets of butter and marmalade, fall-apart white rolls and plastic cheese, manipulated with a super-lightweight plastic knife, and eaten lying down in two inches of cool water. Drink? Just stoop and suck. Now that's a bad meal story.

At 2am in an Alpine hut you groan, and look at the weather, and unfortunately it isn't bad enough to justify going back to bed. You put your feet into wooden 'hut slippers', and eat French bread that squeaks when you bite it. And if you do ever manage to swallow the bread, it's time to face the terrors of the outside toilet...

The Austrians have made an institution of the hut breakfast; they serve it in hotels. It consists of small cups of coffee, stale bread, smoked cheese and salami. There's a choice of bread: you can have stale white bread or, for the echt Bergsteiger or real mountain man, stale rye bread. This menu is designed to get you out and onto the mountain really quickly.

Of course there's also the science side of it – so let's get that out of the way with a small table of contents. Food, for hill people, is fuel, and what counts is calories (or joules, if you're really metric – 4.2 kilojoules is a calorie).

Carbohydrate	4cal/g
Sugar	4cal/g
Fat	9cal/g
Alcohol	7cal/g

If you're pulling a month's food behind you on a sledge then you want a high-fat diet. The rest of us can't quite stomach stirring an ounce of butter into the evening cocoa as Scott did in the Antarctic. Our diet will consist of carbohydrate (fairly slow-release fuel), sugar (quick-release fuel) and as much fat as we can bear.

When it comes to food, it actually doesn't matter how much or how little cash you spend. The intensively researched, marketed and packed sports energy bar really does have almost as many calories as the same weight of custard cream biscuits.

Leaving aside obviously wet food such as oranges, most of the things you put in your rucksack come in at between 4 and 5 calories per gram. This applies to dehydrated suppers and cheese sandwiches, powdered soup, oatmeal, apple tartlets, pork pies and muesli bars.

A long day of hardish walking requires 4000 calories. If you start off unfit and with unsightly personal bulges you won't need as much as that to start with – although on the whole the bulges are just going to slip down into the backs of the legs. So the convenient calculation is: about 1kg of food a day – or, in old-fashioned, 2lb.

A stove is a luxury. You'd get more heat into you by eating the fuel blocks. As water is abundant on British hills it need not be carried in the form of lunch. Sugar should not be the basic food: large chunks of chocolate lead to sudden energy surges followed by famished reaction. Healthy food with vitamins is heavy and doesn't travel well: I do a lot of healthy eating on shop doorsteps. Suitable food for carrying will be starchy carbohydrate in a fairly dry form at four calories per gram, with some sugar and fat to improve the ratios. Which means almost anything, really.

Fast Food

The famous fellrunner Joss Naylor does Lakeland hills in clumps of a dozen powered by his wife's rock buns. Martin Moran, who holds the record for the Munros in winter and also for the Alpine 4000m peaks non-stop, favours honey sandwiches on wholemeal bread. My running companion Glyn Jones has cleverly calculated that custard cream biscuits have the same calories per gram as Mars bars at a quarter of the cost. Anne Stentiford was not just the fastest woman over the 47 peaks of the Buckley Round in Snowdonia – she was the fastest person. She did 61 miles and 8800m/29,000ft of ascent in 19 hours 19 minutes, on satsumas and Mr Kipling's Bramley apple tartlets. Satsumas are just wasteful water, but then she wasn't carrying her own luggage.

Mike Thompson, food mastermind on Everest 1975, says simply, 'The most important thing about food is that there should be some'.

However, almost as important is that you should be able to eat it. Malcolm Mclachlan attempted a nasty but instructive run: the self-supported Southern Upland Way, carrying food for the entire route over the length of the entire route.

His schedule and food supplies were for three and a half days for the 210 fairly hilly miles. He made a slight mistake with his bivvybag: its bright orange colour attracted the young people of Melrose, who wondered if he was rubbish that ought to be thrown into the river. His more serious mistake was his food: ready-wrapped meals of oatmeal muesli (400 cal/100g, fine so far) with a little dried fruit, rendered tempting and flavoursome with – nothing at all. After two and a half days he couldn't face it, far less stomach it, and ended up throwing away food that he had carried 150 miles and that he needed.

The only successful unsupported SU Way has been a winter one, by Glyn Jones. Glyn takes the pleasures of abstinence further than most, and a full account of this particular journey makes distressing reading. He did not carry a sleeping bag, reckoning that the same weight in extra clothes would be just as warm at night and more useful during the daytime. He did not carry a bivvy, by the same reckoning: an opened-out fertiliser bag could be both bivvy and daytime cape. Afterwards, however, he conceded that a proper bag 'would have made the nights bearable'. He started with 6kg/14lb of high-calorie food which he supplemented with rosehips gathered from the November hedges; and finished six days and five hours later with just 50g/2oz of oatmeal and cheese.

'Being a back-to-basics man I wanted to prove that, even at the end of this most technological century, a journey in winter could be successfully made without high-tech gear. I hoped it would also illustrate another of my favourite tenets: you can still obtain some of the atmosphere of 19th-century exploration in tame old Britain if the criteria are stern enough.'

Stripped for action: hill-runners minimise gear for the sake of speed

High Cuisine

At 7000m/23,000ft on Annapurna, Bonington and Whillans found their snowhole larder stocked with whisky, sausages and – that's it. Whisky, sausages. After two days they came up with the obvious recipe: sausages flambéed in whisky.

Here's an even sadder story. On an earlier trip Glyn ran out of custard creams under Ben Alder, but that didn't matter. At Dalwhinnie is a lovely shop run by Mrs McLean – she once sold me a whole smoked chicken. Glyn ran out along Loch Ericht for 12 miles to find – no shop. Mrs McLean had died two months before.

Dalwhinnie is the highest village in the Highlands, and also the most dismal. Rain thrown off the A9 by large lorries scoots across the moor for hundreds of yards before spattering into a peatpool. In all Dalwhinnie, Glyn found or scrounged a kilogram of white sugar and half a loaf of sliced white bread. On these he crossed Cairn Toul, Braeriach, Ben Macdui and Cairngorm. Two days later he turned the sugar bag inside out to lick the corners and trotted down to Donside.

These were meals of inconvenience; given the choice, what Bonington goes for is the bar supper at the Mill Inn, Mungrisedale. However, diets just as dodgy have been taken from conviction and personal taste. Hugh Symonds ran the Munros in 66 summer days on Christmas puddings mostly. But on Kanchenjunga, in 1930, a climber called Irwin Schneider… (you aren't going to believe this, so I'll look it up. It's in Frank Smythe's *The Mountain Scene*, Adam and Charles Black, 1938, page 110; the expedition was led by Professor Dyhrenfurth) …used to eat Christmas pudding dampened down with Worcester sauce and mayonnaise. He used to eat this for breakfast. Frank Smythe took a picture of him doing it.

I prefer not to linger over a material called 'pork block' included in army Compo rations in the sixties. An early experiment in dehydrated food, this could be nibbled straight from the packet, when it tasted like cotton wool. Alternatively, it could be reconstituted in hot water for five minutes, and then it tasted like hot wet cotton wool.

Likewise let us pass over pemmican (a form of leather supposedly edible) and settle for a moment on tsampa. I suspect that tsampa is actually a result of Sherpa ingenuity. Instead of saying, 'Sorry, that's what happens when you accidentally drop a rucksack into the Dudh Kosi torrent', a wily porter came up with, 'But this is what we eat in

THE ART OF LIGHTWEIGHT LONG-DISTANCE

Nepal. Speciality of the region. You don't mean to say you actually meant me to keep the tea, the butter and the oatmeal in separate packages?' And then came one of the truly great throwaway lines: 'Of course, it ought to be rancid yak butter really…'.

Dr Hans Blodig of Switzerland studied the calorific figures given above and came to a starkly simple conclusion. A kilogram of butter has 50 per cent more calories than a kilogram of sandwiches. Dr Blodig was the first person to ascend every one of the Alpine 4000m/13,000ft peaks, and he washed down his all-butter diet with neat alcohol (at 7cal/g).

Let's slip in another simple recipe. Glacier sorbet. Ingredient: a little plastic tub of Swiss jam. Hero brand, black cherry, is a good one. Method: empty the jam onto a snowfield, carefully avoiding crevasses. Using the spike of an ice axe, stir the snowfield. Simple, but effective.

Mountain meals are food with altitude: sausages fried with tinned pineapple in a lay-by on the A9; the night my father came back from the Kingshouse and found the Lagangarbh stove red hot, with the stew a layer of black grease on the walls of the hut and his sleeping bag; the compacted cheese-Marmite-honey sandwich. At the same time there's the two inches of whisky left by some booted philanthropist at the Feshie bothy. There's Church Hall fruitcake served at midnight by the Long Distance Walkers' Association. Or there's an orange against a deep blue sky, as it passes in a high parabola across a frozen Perthshire bog from my friend Colin's dry boulder to my dry boulder 10 yards away.

And just sometimes, on a sunset summit, there's the mashed potato of the gods. Ben More Mull, it was, and we'd climbed with our bivvybags into grey drizzle expecting a night of interesting misery. Fifty feet below the Cioch we emerged into evening sunlight, and scrambled the rock-ridge looking down on swirling cloud and the Atlantic. The mash was the sophisticated sort, with little green bits, and we sat and ate it with plastic spoons as the lighthouses came on from Oban to Benbecula. Iona swam away in a silver haze, the sea went purple and so did the sky, and the moon came up from beyond the other side of Scotland. We finished up our potatoes, left the washing-up for a lower altitude and unrolled our bags within the stone ring of the summit cairn.

'It's not what you eat. It's where you eat it.'

MOUNTAINS UNDER THE MOON

It's a very natural thing, when you're young and inexperienced, to be afraid of the dark. As a cold spring day turns slowly colder and surrounding mountains take on the golden glow of departing day, you hold up fingers between the sun and the horizon and realise that three fingers times five minutes means only another quarter of an hour.

At this point you start to walk rather fast. Fast walking is enjoyable in itself, when you're only doing it for another half-hour, and speed doesn't mean sweaty shirts but only a toasty glow in the ever chillier air. With the grey spectre of night-time creeping up out of the valleys, friends stop wanting to hang around working out which is Yr Aran – no, I meant the other Yr Aran. For once, they're quite content to join you in the sort of vigorous walking they'd normally sneer at. You bundle down the path towards the car park, slightly out of control, inflicting a bit of a bashing on toes that, after all, won't be needed again till next weekend.

You arrive at the Pen-y-Grwyd panting and smiling. Look out through the steamy windows and the world outside's gone quite dark. You may be congratulating yourself on having used up all the day there was.

Then one day you're with an older, supposedly wiser, walker – and the wiser walker says it's such a lovely evening, why don't we wander off over Yr Aran itself on the way down? Well, because it'll mean rather a lot of vigorous path-bashing to beat out the ending of the day, but if the old fellow's game then why not? But the old fellow ambles on the same as always, and once on Yr Aran wants to sit around on that handy fallen wall identifying the lighthouses of Anglesey. So you point out that if the lighthouses are alight it must be night-time, but he tells you not to worry as there's going to be a moon, and what's this, you don't have a torch? What an odd thing, if you can afford that fancy jacket and the GPS and all, you ought to have been able to fix yourself up with a torch…

There are certain thresholds in hillwalking: you step across them into a new world. There's the day when you say stuff the guidebook, even stuff dear old Alfred Wainwright himself, and set off on a route you've made up all on your own off the map. There's the afternoon when the cloud drops but you find your way down to Edale anyway. There's when you decide to do Sharp Edge the rocky way above the frightful drop. And there's the day when you deliberately walk on into the night.

Dark is certainly different. Dodgy? Not if you've got a bivvybag. But is it fun?

Because it wasn't fun at all when I left it too late coming down off Ben Ime, and the slope just got steeper as the light went, and I could see all the cars with their headlights and heaters on driving over Rest and Be Thankful towards teatime. The ground was frozen, and downhill in the dark was making my toes hurt, and I couldn't work out which way was the ridge. And then there was a black place at the other end of my torchlight and I was at the top of some cliffs. To left here or to right? The map is hard to read in the dark, but it's going to go on being dark for another 12 hours, so I head right, towards the sound of the rushing stream, and those crags are still down there somewhere, so I'm digging the ice axe into the wet grass in a nervous, unhappy way.

Mountain under the moon: Buachaille Etive Mor

In the darkness this side of the rushing stream was brushwood from a former forest. Once I'd fallen over twice in a single step I needed out of the brushwood. Stone-to-stone in the dark is pretty silly, so it was thigh-deep through the stream very slowly with the ice axe.

And down at the bottom, there seemed to be a river between me and my car.

This sort of fun can only be enjoyed afterwards, and hard work even then. But it's different when you do the darkness deliberately and towards a bivvy. For one thing, you aren't doing it downhill…

You could be coming up out of Eskdale with a Woolpack barmeal inside you. There are a few larch trees along the near horizon, the stars are above and the squelching boot-sounds are below. And then it flattens and goes snowy, and there's the view down on Wastwater. On no other lake is there quite such a diving-board viewpoint as Whin Rigg. From the summit to the water's edge is 600 yards sideways, and over 450m/1500ft of drop.

Up on Whin Rigg, on a February teatime, you discover why writers 200 years ago found Wastwater the scariest lake. Snow lies along the ridge, snow that's crisping up as the day's warmth streams into the night. The Wasdale mountains stand sharp against the stars. Down through the gaps of Broad Crag are concentrated glimpses of Wastwater. On the land no lights show, and the lake is black. There's the youth hostel, shut till springtime, its lawn pale in the moonlight. Two steps sideways, though, and you're looking down onto the black tangle of Low Wood. And to zoom in on that view, simply take a short walk to the northwest – exactly 10 seconds later you'll see Wastwater in intimate close-up…

Snow under the full moon hardly counts as night-time at all: it's a sunny afternoon, except that the snow's crisper and the scenery's in black and white instead of colour. Rather different is when there's a cloud across the moon and stones, rather than snow, underfoot.

Rather different, but still, rather enjoyable. For a long time the stones are pale blobs that you can weave your feet around and not bash your boot-toes at all – and you think, this darkness isn't as black as it's painted. Then you notice that though you can see the stones you can't see the path… So you switch on the torch, and there's a black soggy spot that's been trodden on, and scratched rock beyond, so that's OK. And let's not worry about what happens if the path disappears again and doesn't come back; let's not worry about whether you packed the spare batteries…

Earlier you were trying to get across Hart Fell rather fast during the last of the daylight. And it may still be only six o'clock, but when it gets dark the human brain starts to think sleepy-time. Which may be why the brain strangely doesn't want to worry about those worrying things. It's quite content to occupy the centre of a small pool of torchlight, watching the grass stems go by, looking out for trampled bits of peat and scratches on the rocks.

Lakeland, at night, in winter, is not a busy place. Every 10 minutes a car wanders along the valley floor like a questing glow-worm. The lights of the inn reflect in Brotherswater, and far away is an orange glow that must be Penrith. And then, before you really wanted them to, leaves are rustling overhead, the path is broad and easy, and a black hump ahead is the last car in the car park.

Climb in, switch on the heater, switch on the stereo. Switch on, with real sadness, the headlamps. That's Lakeland away for another weekend.

Nightfall on Cairnsmore of Carsphairn

LARKS IN THE DARK

- Do it alone for the full effect of the primal terrors, but take a friend the first time.

- Pack some spare batteries.

- Uphill is generally OK unless it's boulders or scree. But choose easy routes for the descent (grass or clear path). With the bivvybag, you can sleep on top and leave the downhill till tomorrow.

- Quite big paths can vanish in the dark because of the lack of colour clues.

- There's no point in hurrying; you just fall over. But then, there's no need to hurry. In the daytime you were hurrying because you wanted to get off the hill before dark…

- Night-walking is both slow and cold. Wear extra clothes.

- Understand the moon. The full moon rises at sunset and is in the sky all night. In the week before the full moon, it's usefully bright, and is in the sky during the first part of the night. In the week after the full moon, it doesn't rise till part way through the night. During the week either side of New Moon it's either unhelpfully dim or not there at all.

DAY 0	FULL MOON	In sky all night – bright
DAY 7	3rd QUARTER	Sets at midnight – fairly bright
DAY 14	NEW MOON	Rises at sunrise, sets at sunset – very dim
DAY 21	1st QUARTER	Rises at midnight – fairly bright
DAY 28	FULL MOON again	

The moon rises (and sets) about an hour later than it did the previous night.

Chapter 8

BAG PLANS

'The night proved intensely cold. The clouds had prevented any sunshine reaching the plateau, and the small pools of water and patches of snow, even when we first reached it, were still hard frozen from the previous night's frost. These icy rocks below and a keen north wind above seemed to freeze us to the very marrow, and we shivered with the pain of cold under our scanty rugs. We were all glad when it was time to be moving, and at the first hint of dawn (4.15am) we began to scramble up the rocks and along the ridge leading towards the snow arête.'

A.F. Mummery First ascent Zmutt Ridge Matterhorn, 1879

1 BIVVYBAGGING THE WAINWRIGHTS

The Wainwrights ought to be a project for a lifetime. But all over Lakeland there are people doing five or even ten in a weekend. Profligate, spendthrift souls! Don't they know there are only 315 of the things?

Actually there are only 314 of them – unless, as I do but A.W. doesn't, you include Pillar Rock. Pillar Rock is certainly as Wainwrightworthy as Tarn Crag, Easedale or Grike. And every hill list deserves its difficult one to lift us out of our pedestrian rut into the scary heights of the rockface grapple.

But even Pillar Rock shouldn't take up more than 10 or 20 years of dithering and hesitation; 314 or 315 – what are we going to do when they're all used up?

Well, this being Lakeland, we can climb them again by a different and even better route – and then by a third route that's even better than that. Helvellyn has 17 different ways, and there are still some interesting gills on the west side to have a look at. We can climb them in winter, at night, on skis. But for a real lifetime project, why not bag them in the bag? You haven't really done a Wainwright until you've slept on it.

Any sport requires rules so here are a few for the bivvybagging of the Wainwrights.

1   You must be on the actual summit for sunset, or sunrise, or both.

2   You must bivvy close to the summit, but a reasonable descent of say 30m/100ft vertical (three contours) is allowed.

3   You must actually fall asleep.

4   Tents don't count.

5   barmeal beforehand is a sign of sophistication.

Some descent off the summit is permitted because, unless we can get down out of the wind, it won't be possible to obey the rule about falling asleep. Also, there are some summits which are too narrow to make adequate bedrooms. Cofa Fell may not be a Wainwright but Steeple certainly is – and the top rock of Helm Crag is no place for sleepwalkers.

On the other hand, the lesser Wainwrights offer bedspace for you and several dozen sleeping companions in heatherbed luxury.

Gowbarrow Fell has rocky nooks with shelter from any wind, and from it you get sunset behind Skiddaw, the last steamer nostalgically tracing its wake through water gone all streaky-silver in the late light, and deep heather to lie down on. And in the morning, the sun rises over Ullswater like molten gold from a furnace. Sheffield Pike is better, because the same sunrise is seen from higher up.

My first idea had been for a bivvy at Foxes Tarn, but night caught me on Great Gable and left a choice of scree to sleep on or a descent of the Breast Path in misty torchlight. The scree was altogether too stony for one travelling light without a mat. Sadly, I turned my sore toes towards the Breast Path's thousand feet of steep wet boulders.

But in misted torchlight, even the Breast Path can be lost; and I found myself standing below a small crag on a patch of lumpy lawn. My body fitted among the lumps like a ski-line through a mogulfield.

Low cloud and a sheltered site meant warmth: I could enjoy the luxury of removing the wet waterproofs before getting into bed. I drew the bag over my head and draped it so that the raindrops trickled down the far side of one of the turfy lumps. And a last look outside showed dim crag and boulder, and a brief parting of the clouds. There, for 10 long seconds, was the Great Gable view, down over the tops of the Napes buttresses to the field patterns of Wasdale Head, and the gleam of Wastwater below the Screes.

That lumpy lawn is somewhere within five minutes' sorefoot stumble of Gable summit. But coming back in daylight, I have not been able to find it.

Is there, we wonder, a similar soft spot anywhere on the plateau of Scafell Pike or Bowfell? Kirk Fell and Dow have rounded gravelly tops: one could go down a little to find longer grass and lose the breeze, but that would be to have the view in only one direction. And greed alone should insist on seeing not just sunset or sunrise, not just the Atlantic or Coniston Water, but all four.

The sharp-eyed pedant may have noticed that it's actually possible to bivvybag two separate tops in a single night within Rules 1 and 2. See sunset from Hallin Fell: put small stones under the foam mat to ensure a short sleep, then cross in the dark to Mardale Ill Bell. Fall asleep for a second time, and wake to watch the sun rise over Haweswater reservoir. Well, if you're in such a tearing hurry, then do it that way. Not every top has a lake both sides for the sun to reflect in, and it could also be a way of warming up halfway through.

Rule 5 mentions barmeals. There are two benefits from the barmeal option. It's a shame to walk 15 vigorous hours, rise onto Gibson Knott as the light goes golden, carefully choose a grassy hollow with a view of the village – and then fall asleep within 10 seconds. The supper stop slows you down.

The other advantage is moral and social. From Diogenes onwards, those who sleep out of doors in small containers have been seen as austere nutters who don't have any fun. But people who spend good money on beer – when they could be in a breeze even more bitter than Jennings or Coniston, nibbling muesli bars in gloved hands – such people could almost be described as sensible, surely?

While only one of Lakeland's inns (the Kirkstone) is usefully high, lots of Lakeland's hills are usefully low. Gowbarrow Fell is only 30 minutes above the Royal Dockray – hardly far enough to warm up.

Any barmeal, followed by any hilltop, makes an excellent evening. However, connoisseurs will want to discriminate between the good and the altogether excellent. A low hill – and in particular a low heathery hill – for comfort; but a high hill for the view. However, there are low hills with view, and all of them conveniently listed in Wainwright. A lake to the northwest, for the sunset; or to the northeast, for the dawn. An easy path, or a grassy slope not unbearably steep, for the approach. And in case it gets nasty in the night, either rocky hollows or an easy lee slope to flee down.

Water is not important. You can carry up to half a litre for the evening, and walk downhill to breakfast.

Burgundy with the steak, dry white with the fish, and a good port with the stilton. Here are a few classic combinations of inn and up:

Dining Room	Bedroom	Notes
Wasdale Head Hotel	Scafell	Summer daylight needed
Langstrath Inn	Allen Crags	Via Angle Tarn
Royal Inn, Dockray	Sheffield Pike	Daylight needed for Glencoyne head
Fish, Buttermere	Haystacks	Good heather
	Fleetwith Pike	Sunset over Crummock Water
Kirkstone Inn	Red Screes	But get up there before dark
Howtown Hotel	Place Fell	Path losable in dark
Screes, Nether Wasdale	Middle Fell	Compasswork needed to stay on ridge
Traveller's Rest, Grasmere	Easedale Tarn	Waterfalls in the dark

Keswick (any)	Skiddaw	Easy climb but hard bed
Dungeon Ghyll	Rossett Pike	Or Angle Tarn for shelter
Sun Inn Coniston	Blind Tarn	Sunrise beyond two lakes
Newfield Inn Seathwaite	Low Crag	Cragtop site with heather
Tan Hill Inn	Nine Standards	Good peat hollow at summit

2 BAG AND CAMERA

There used to be a motto of a factory that made matches in East Africa: 'A good one in every box'. Pictures that look great through the viewfinder evaporate somewhere on their long journey down the lens, onto the film, and through the mysterious vats of the photo lab. Landscape turns flat, telephone poles leap into the front of the composition, fellow-walkers take on awkward and ungainly poses. Too often we have to console ourselves with the motto: 'A good one on every roll'.

Place the feet in a firm but comfortable position; breathe out, and relax; and then **don't** press the shutter button. With experience we learn this simple sequence of movements. Just by not taking the hazy afternoon landscape, the harshly lit and squinting friend, the motor-car foreground, we can get the success rate up to five or six good ones on a roll.

Wouldn't it be nice if there were a single piece of equipment, costing £50 to £100, that could get your good-one count up to 15 or 20 per roll? If you could go into the shop and say, 'I'm taking too many boring pictures and not enough good ones,' and they answered, 'Ah yes Madam (or Sir), a lot of people have that problem. What you want is a Binary Autofocus Grabber, or BAG.'

The BAG exists. It is made of strong, breathable Gore-tex. It isn't a bag for putting the camera in; it's rather too big for that purpose, being two metres long. It's the bag for putting yourself in.

The one really good time for taking pictures on hilltops is just before you get to the hilltops in the early morning. The other really good time is just after you've gone away in the evening. We're not just talking sunsets and sunrises – though there is something very satisfying

Ullswater dawn from Sheffield Pike

indeed in a matched pair. The sun goes down behind Arran, and seven hours later, up it comes again behind the Southern Uplands.

During the main part of the day, overhead light does its best to flatten the landscape, and even if a good scene should appear, walking companions hurry you forward before you've had time to get it into the camera. During the hour after sunrise, the chilly air is crystal clear, and sideways light brings out the shapes of the hills. And no companions are going to hurry you forward, because nobody you know wanted to spend the night with you on top of Kirriereoch Hill. With nobody to put into the foreground, you may have to pose an accommodating sheep. There's time to shoot off half a roll (and half of them will be good ones), wander along the ridge, and shoot off the rest of the roll.

At high noon, the least uninteresting pictures are often those taken towards the sun – using some expedient to shade the lens. In the late afternoon, I instinctively turn the lens side-on to the sun. This makes the most of the long shadows lying across the slope. Later on, even pictures directly away from the sun can be good because of the golden tones. As the daylight changes, the eye adjusts to compensate – but the camera doesn't. Thus the photo can show a beautiful evening glow you weren't aware of during the actual evening.

And then it's time to turn right round and start shooting into the setting sun.

But why is the sunset when you're in it so much better than the sunset when you get it back from the developer and stick it in the album?

The best sunset I ever saw was from Hallin Fell, above Ullswater. I spent the day on Helvellyn, and came down Striding Edge in the snow. I had a nice hot meal in Glenridding, and walked that lovely lakeside path in the golden afternoon, then started up Hallin Fell. Halfway up I stopped to take pictures of the sky as it went yellow behind Helvellyn, and thought, 'great, that's me got the sunset'. So I went on, and then I realised that the sunset had finished going yellow behind Helvellyn just to give itself room to go red all over. It looked like the underside of a feather bed when a really large king has just been murdered on the top. And that black streak, heading up towards top right: that had to be the shadow of Grasmoor, thrown upwards from behind the horizon. Amazing!

The best sunset I ever saw – but not the best I ever photographed. What went wrong?

The eyes that look at my Hallin Fell photos have not just done Striding Edge in the snow and gone rather fast up Hallin Fell. They haven't got the cool evening air on their face, and aren't wondering just how unbearably cold it's going to be in the bivvybag on Hallin Fell in February. All these factors help to make real life more interesting than photographs of it.

When I sat on that evening hill, I saw two beautiful things: the sky and the scenery. The camera, however, can only see one of those things at a time – this is because camera film isn't such clever stuff as the rods and cones in the living eye. Cut my Hallin photo along the skyline and get a picture of Ullswater in very poor light conditions, somewhat underexposed. The bottom half of my sunset is a bad picture.

One I took just above Honister youth hostel has less interesting scenery, and so is a more successful photo. The sides of Honister Pass make simple grey V-shapes, leading the eye to the mauve blob that is Buttermere. But still, if you can't get sky and scenery, it makes more sense to sacrifice the scenery. An automatic camera, left to its own devices, will do this for you: it'll under-expose the sky, which makes the colours even better than they really were, and it'll turn the scenery into a simple black bit at the bottom.

Nature, out there in front of the camera, can be counted on to do something with the sky. This leaves you, behind the camera, to sort out the black bit at the bottom. It looks like scenery, but in the picture it's just going to be a shape. If it's an interesting shape, then you'll get an interesting sunset photo.

One way to make the shape interesting is to poke holes in it. From Honister I wandered up onto Grey Knotts and found a peaty pool with boulders behind. The water carries on the colours of the sunset; black whiskers of grass stick into the pool; and the rocks are rough-edged above. By this time most of the fun had gone out of the sunset. Even so, the black bits were so interesting that this made one of my best-ever sunset photos.

If you're a person, one interesting shape for the black bit below the sunset is another person. Get your fellow-human to make itself into a shape with a hole in – part its legs, or poke out its elbows. Position them so that the bottom ends of the legs, too, stand out against the sky. Only a professional torturer really likes the shape of three-quarters of a person.

Failing a hole, a pool or a person, another way of dealing with the black bit at the bottom is to leave most of it out. Horizon across the middle is a bad idea at any time of day, but if all that's below the horizon is a whole lot of nothing, the horizon should be banging against the lower edge.

Midsummer sun doesn't set in the west, but in the northwest. Are you so presumptuous as to actually go out expecting a wondrous sunset photoshoot? Then bear in mind that if you want it to go down behind the Isle of Skye you need to be in Morar, not Applecross.

Suppose you've any film left after the evening glow and the sunset. You can have some more fun and take photos in the dark. You'll need a camera with the letter B appearing among the shutter-speeds. And you'll need a bit of luck.

A tripod is a help: but who hauls tripods across the hilltops? So hold the camera down firmly on a rock: there'll be some camera movement, but you expect things to be fuzzy in the dark. You can't see the needle of the exposure meter? Well, if your camera's prepared to go along with you, set it to under-expose by two stops – you want the picture to look dark, not like a very bad one taken at midday.

Alternatively, just guess. Set to maximum aperture: f/2.8 on most cameras. At the moment when the first star appears, try an exposure of 10 seconds. When it's completely dark, but moonlit, try a full minute. When it's completely dark, but starlit, try several minutes.

Ice axe and crampons; backpack and mule; campfire, beer and guitar – these are some of the great outdoor combinations. To them I have to add: bivvybag and camera. Nights in bags on hills are uncomfortable and inspiring. They chill the body, but set the spirit alight. They leave pictures embedded in the memory, and pretty good ones on the 100ASA Process Paid as well.

3 CORBETT BAGGING

Where Scottish mountains are concerned, the Munros are done from parked cars mostly. But bivvybagging and Corbett-bagging go together like a Cynic philosopher and his barrel.

Munros are Scottish mountains of over 3000ft/914.4m. There are currently 284 of them in the list first prepared in 1891 by Sir Hugh Munro, Baronet, of Lindertis in Angus. Munro-bagging goes something like this:

0-100: Oh no, I'm not a Munro-bagger, I don't know how many I've done. But I do know that I shan't ever ascend 284 separate Scottish tops.

100-200: I've bought 'Munro's Tables', and the 3000ft tops are coloured with yellow highlighter on my Landranger maps. Oh no, I'm still not a Munro-bagger.

200–283: Still not a Munro-bagger. But realising that the list, formerly impossibly long, is actually rather too short. In the words of Nina Persson of the Cardigans, 'You're losing your favourite game.' Old mountains are always worth revisiting, but the pleasure of arriving on the top of a totally new one will soon be over forever.

284: Certainly not a Munro-bagger as they're all already bagged. What next? Repeat round, or two, or seven. Perhaps not England, but Ireland maybe, or Wales. Or the Corbetts?

The Corbetts are Scottish mountains of heights between 2500ft and 2999ft (762–914.3m). Currently there are 220 of them, from Sutherland to the Southern Uplands, from the Hebrides to Aberdeen. The following Corbetts will feature in anyone's list of Scotland's best: Ben Loyal, The Cobbler, The Merrick, Goatfell, Streap, Beinn Bhan of Applecross, Beinn Dearg Torridon and Beinn Dearg Mor of Letterewe, Foinaven, Garbh Bheinn of Ardgour, Glamaig.

The completed Munroist will probably have done all of these good ones already. For him, the typical Corbett experience will be more like this.

Corbett Day 1

Beinn Liath Mhor a' Ghuibhais Li

Corbetts are small, Corbetts are easy. So this rough heather above Loch Glascarnoch won't bother us long. Except that, oh dear, there's a deer fence. Do we go round, or do we naughtily go over and flounder among new forest ditches? We go round, and rise up the moor at least as steadily as the peat slop rises up our gaiters.

The moor curves over, and the only alcoholic outlet for 30 miles drops out of sight. Into sight rises a mile or two more heather, laid flat and interspersed with black wet bits. Beyond the flat rises more heather to the rounded crest that's almost as wide as its name on the map. 'Liath Mhor a' Ghuibhais Li' is 'Big Grey of a Pinetree Sort of Colour' – fair enough, if pinetrees were to grow up here they would probably be big grey ones.

The top hundred feet of Ghuibhais Li are mildly mountainous, being covered in fine gravel and a few stones. The view from a Corbett, we all know, is a good one. The view from Ghuibhais Li is of the entire Fannich range: nine wonderful Munros, sided with old snow, topped with rock, and linked by sharp exciting ridges – nine fine Munros on none of which we are currently standing. After a couple of hours of reverse flogging across the heather, and a diversion when we hit the other side of that deer fence, the licensed premises come reluctantly back into view. Small Corbetts and whisky go together well, for one's declining years; but after Ghuibhais Li, perhaps even better without the small Corbetts...

Part of the difficulty lies with the list itself.

Munro's table may be eccentric and vague in its criteria. However, the result is an exhilarating mix of famous mountains, long days along the ridges and obscure but interesting corners. Munro's listing has the just the right proportion of the grim and austere among the classics: for every two rocky Mamores, a heather hummock like Meall Chuaich.

Corbett's criterion – 150m/500ft of drop before reaching any higher point – is more sensible but less satisfactory.

Firstly, it eliminates amusing controversy. In 1997, eight new summits suddenly arrived in Munro's Tables. This sort of thing keeps everybody on their toes.

Even more seriously, the 500ft rule means that Corbetts tend to be standoffish and isolated. The standard Munro day goes over several. But chase Corbetts and the bigger hills tend to get in the way. Peter Drummond, writing in *TGO* magazine, has made a calculation from the SMC guidebooks. The average Munro involves 580m/1900ft of ascent and 3.2 miles horizontal. The average Corbett takes 655m/2150ft and an extra half-mile. The 284 big Munros take 150 hill days; the 220 smaller Corbetts take 170.

There's another reason why smaller, in Scottish mountain terms, is bigger. And it also can be stated statistically. Over 2000 people have done the 288 Munros. At the last count, just 146 had done the Corbetts. A Munro has a large path, eroded in places until rebuilt in chunks of stone by the National Trust. A Corbett has no path at all. Every step you take you're deciding which side of the tussock has the bog, which ridge is on the right mountain, and whether you're lost yet. When you come off any Corbett onto any Munro you hit the Munro-baggers' path. You relax, switch off the brain and stride out. Sgurr na Ciche (1040m/3400ft) is a fine craggy hill, but you never have to wonder whether the rock you're about to climb is actually climbable – trample marks and scratching show you the way. But down on Beinn Aden (887m/2900ft) bare rock is mossy and untrodden, and what isn't bare rock is swamp.

The Corbetts, then, are not a second-best for the elderly. My own plan – and I urge anyone passing the 100-Munro mark to adopt it – is to start the Corbett campaign much earlier. They should be used to prolong one's completion of the Munros themselves.

There is a risk. Dawdling over the Corbetts may mean not completing the Munros at all. But the beauty of a lifetime project is this: you don't actually fail until the moment of death. After which point, you're no longer in a position to care. Well, we have to assume that the Heavenly Ranges are even better than those of mainland Scotland...

Here are three different days you get if you start the Corbett-bagging straight away:

Corbett Day 2

Not Cleaning the Self-Catering

For the rest of the party, the rainy final day of a short break at Kingshouse meant getting up at nine, cleaning the self-catering, and driving down the A82. I got up at six and made a quick, wet crossing of Beinn a' Chrulaiste. These 600m/2000ft of stones and grass are no

The hard one: The Cobbler

Green Crag sunset

Grey Knotts summit after sunset

Dentdale dawn, at the end of the Pennine journey

substitute for Buachaille Etive Beag or Bidean. But as a way of making you late for cabin-cleaning duties, just the thing. The Buachaille and the many pools of Rannoch Moor appeared through holes in the mist, and all the way past Loch Lomond to Glasgow I had damp hair and the virtuous feeling of having bagged a whole hill before breakfast.

CORBETT DAY 3

Section 10A

Section 10A is Morvern, Sunart, Ardgour and Moidart. It has 16 Corbetts, and not a Munro. Here is the place where you can walk Corbett to Corbett along the high ridges – and what Corbetts they are too. Fuar Bheinn and Garbh Bheinn and Rois-bheinn; Ben Resipol and Sgurr Dhomhnuill. Among these grassy hollows you unroll the bivvybag at dusk, and watch the Isle of Rum turn pink, then purple, then black in the middle of a silvery sea. If that sea dropped 150m/500ft, this would become one of the main Munro places. Do you really want to save them for your decrepitude, and do them one at a time from sea level?

CORBETT DAY 4

Little and Large

Three Munros make a good tough day, but one Munro and a Corbett is tougher. Ben Ime is a long gentle slope up out of Arrochar, past the Narnain boulders and under the crags of the Cobbler. That's the way the path goes, anyway; and the path should know.

But suppose you're also after Beinn Luibheinn. Ben Ime now suddenly turns into a long amble up a neglected valley, and a rather nice ridge that sticks out in the general direction of Ben Lui. Ime's final cone is surprisingly steep – there may be a path somewhere under the snow but probably isn't.

At the top are some footprints. The footprints have come up the long gentle path from Arrochar, turned round, and gone back down it again. The footprints never realised that in every direction but one, Ime is steep, rather craggy, and mostly mountain. For now – ah, the interesting bit – we have to cross to Luibheinn. No path joins Corbett to Munro, and nor does any guidebook. (There are Corbett guidebooks, but they do the Corbetts one at a time or with other Corbetts.) Head down the gentle footprints until the slope on the right stops being steep and savage, bear off down snowy hollows between bare rocks, and get involved in steep and savage anyway.

Beinn Luibheinn's a fairly ordinary Corbett. It has a few acres of craggy plateau – its name amusingly translates as 'Cowhill Hill' – and its summit is proper rocks. It's below the cloud when Ime and Narnain are up and in it. At sunset, wisps of pink mist are parting to reveal the bracelet of headlights around the base of Beinn an Lochain.

Ime alone would never have taken long enough to have you coming down again in the dark...

The aim of the game isn't to be easy. The aim of the game isn't to be totally tough. The aim of the game is to be a game. What with cars, breathable fabrics and replacement titanium knees, the Munro game is no longer enough for the average lifetime. When tennis players get too good at it, they raise the net. For the game of Scottish mountains, the answer is rather to lower it, catching Corbetts as well. And Corbetts not afterwards, but during.

The aim, indeed, is to triumphantly complete both lists at once in a single day at the age of 83. Just now, with 220 Munros and only 60 Corbetts already visited, I'm paying my respects to the heathery east. Meantime, I'm laying aside some of the finer hills (Beinn Lair, Ben Lui) for my old age. And some time later in the century, I hope you'll see me sadly passing above Loch an Daimh on my way between Meall Buidhe (932m/3057ft) and Meall Buidhe (910m/2985ft) – and wondering what to do with the remaining years between ages 85 and 100.

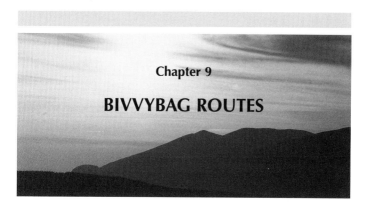

Chapter 9

BIVVYBAG ROUTES

1: SLEEPING ON SKIDDAW

Start/Finish:	Car parking at Peter House Farm, GR250323
Distance:	17 miles/27km
Ascent:	1500m/5000ft
Approx. walking time:	10½ hours
Terrain:	Grassy hillsides and paths
Map:	Double-sided (recent version of) Outdoor Leisure 4 if you wish to include the final field bridleway
Refreshments:	Sun Inn, Bassenthwaite Village
Public transport:	Buses Keswick/Carlisle to Bassenthwaite Village turnoff

The Route:

Road leads north for a mile past Horsemoor Hills to bridleway track on the right. Cross Great Cockup to narrow pass (meltwater channel) of Trusmadoor. Just down right, the gap of Frozenfell Gill leads in towards Great Sca Fell and Knott. Head for a stile at fence corner before Little Calva (GR284317). A small path with fence on its right leads down to the top of Whitewater Dash.

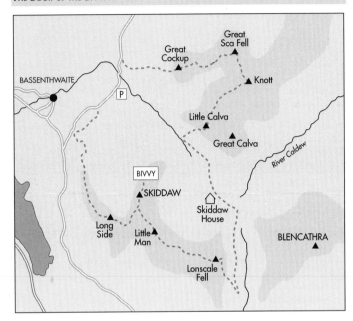

Turn left on wide track (Cumbria Way) past Skiddaw House. Where the main path turns down left towards Glenderaterra Beck (GR293279) the smaller path of the Cumbria Way continues ahead, contouring along the steep valley side below Lonscale Crags. After a mile it emerges from the valley to a sudden view and a fence.

Head straight up onto Lonscale Fell – the 703m/2300ft East Top is worth visiting. A small path and fence, easy even in the dark, lead over Jenkin Hill to the Pony Path. Cross at a gateway to include Little Man on the way to Skiddaw. Skiddaw summit is stony and windy, with ineffective shelter cairns. Descend north a short way to find grass to lie on.   *(12½ miles, 1430m/4700ft, 8 hours)*

Return southwards past the summit for 100 yards to the next slight rise with shelter cairn. A cairned path slants down right to Carlside Tarn (often dry). Descend the fine ridge of Longside Edge, and at its foot drop right, to a track. This leads round left, with ladder stiles, then bridleway arrows point down alongside remains of a hedge. Turn

Frozenfell Gill, at the Back o' Skiddaw

left to the road, or right on bridleway with some waymarks past Barkbeth to join road near Melbecks.

They say that Lakeland is too busy. But there is a way to avoid the crowds, and it's simply to be there when the crowds aren't.

Most walkers leave their cars at about 10 o'clock and come back about four in the afternoon. So just do the opposite. Leave the car at four in the afternoon and come back at 10 the next day.

This has many advantages. You can arrive by bus or even a lake ferry – public transport runs through the middle of the day; just right for overnight walkers. You're out under the evening light, and the rising of the sun. You get a nice long sleep in your bivvybag before the tiresome business of coming back down off your mountain. And you reach the road well rested, ready for the haul back along the A66.

There are also, it is true, certain disadvantages. Even when the first hill you've got your eye on isn't Great Cockup. Which in my case was.

Cockup itself was no mistake. The grassy slope was steep to start with – but who suffers from early-morning stiffness at four in the afternoon? The last party of day walkers came down past me. Their

101

group was strangely spread out, and slow; indeed, it seemed to consist entirely of stragglers. Long and soft is the walking at the back of Skiddaw. These rounded mounds of grass, peat and gravel tempt you ever forward in hope of eventually reaching somewhere exciting.

Not to be bored at the Back o' Skiddaw: this was my ambitious plan for the afternoon.

The views were afternoon haze, and the nearest rocky place was Carrock Fell (too far). If you can't find a hill try a hole, so I dropped into Frozenfell Gill. Now the unexciting grass was up above my head. Down where I was, shale dropped into a rocky stream. Me and the stream wiggled about in our hollow; no idea where we were really, some unidentifiable slice of Skiddaw out behind and a small waterfall ahead.

Back up on the grasslands, the view had shifted round slightly and become less hazy. These are humorous hills. Off on the left, Brae Fell means 'Hill Hill' and recalls the mythic and probably non-existent Pen-y-Beacon Hill ('Hill Hill Hill') on the Welsh border. While ahead, Great Sca Fell cocks a snook at the presumably un-Great Scafell above Wasdale Head. It's a very small snook – Great Sca Fell has only two little contour lines to call its own.

Fences, heather and a bit of peat – let's get onto the main business of the day. The main business of this particular day was to be the night. I headed southwards along the Cumbria Way, creeping past the windows of the youth hostel to see Keswick switch on its lights. I reached Lonscale Fell at the grey moment of the day.

At the grey moment you either get out the torch or put the map away. The air turns cool so you can go as fast as you like without getting sweaty. And fast is what you do like, with Skiddaw still two hours ahead and night quite a bit closer than that.

So I put the map away, for who can get lost on Lonscale? On the right, Skiddaw Forest was a pit of darkness that with a little imagination might still contain trees, wolves and wild boar. What dark shape disturbs the YHA dustbin? Lean forward over your bubbling Vesta curry (Skiddaw House is still self-catering) and see a sinister nose pressed against the dark windowpane… Must try Skiddaw House some time.

No bubbling Vesta for me. All I had to warm my battered pork pie over were the flickering streetlights of Keswick, with the silvery aluminium saucepan of Derwentwater poised above. Ahead, a band of dirty orange streaked the horizon. Time, after hanging in a grey limbo all along Jenkin Hill, suddenly speeded up. The gate on the Pony Path loomed up out of some quite thick darkness. The path beyond was a grey streak; the cairn on Little Man a black shape against slightly lighter black.

I stopped to enjoy the last of the orange light with the cone of Long Side for foreground. Then clouds rose to wrap me in a damp black blanket. Chilly rain from behind, a somewhat sleepy brain, and one patch of torchlight on damp stones being very like another: there's a strong feeling of not being anywhere in particular. Is this what a ghost feels like, passing through the world without ever actually existing in it? The trig and indicator suddenly indicate a particular place. The Top.

Skiddaw is the most night-visited summit. Every year 250 contenders in the Four Tops Challenge touch the trig before turning briskly back towards the Pony Path. Bob Graham Round runners turn right to bounce down through the invisible heather. Do it boing! boing! like Zebedee in *The Magic Roundabout*, relax and be happy: there are 41 more hills ahead to be miserable over…

On 21st August 1815, a party including the Wordsworths, Robert Southey, James Boswell (son of Dr Johnson's biographer) and a dozen others celebrated the victory of Waterloo with an overnight bonfire party on Skiddaw. 'We roasted beef and boiled plum-puddings there; sung "God save the King" round the most furious body of flaming tar-barrels; fired cannon at every health and rolled large blazing balls of tow and turpentine down the steep side of the mountain,' wrote Southey in his diary.

In the excitement the kettle fell over into the fire. A serious loss: the revellers would now have to drink their rum neat. Wordsworth himself was the culprit, and the partygoers gathered round him in mocking song: 'Twas you that kicked the kettle down! Twas you Sir, you!' Oddly, this little episode did not get transcribed into *The Prelude*.

No flaming tar barrels tonight. I headed on northwards, looking for less wind, fewer stones and a break in the brisk shower. These I found some 200 yards north of the summit.

Now, there are times when you lie in your sleeping bag, warm and cosy, feeling the raindrops as they hit the other side of the breathable green, and sure of waking up at daylight still dry and alive. And there are times when you lie in the same bag feeling almost sure. These two sorts of times are quite, quite different – even though they may be separated by the mere flicker of an instant. That's when that flicker of an instant is also a flicker of lightning.

Earlier in the summer I'd seen a line of ploughed-up earth where lightning had torn open a Scottish hill ridge. Now, in theory, lightning travels around the outside surface of a wet bivvybag. In theory also...

It flickered again. Drumming of rain on the nylon above my nose drowned out any thunder. Not all that close, then.

Where was I? On a broad ridge of Skiddaw in a downpour in the dark. Was I about to unbag into the rain and walk downhill, getting all my nice warm nightwear soaking wet? I was not. With that decided, and perhaps surprisingly, I simply fell asleep.

In the morning it wasn't thunderstorming any more. However, it was still raining. I unzipped a small opening and brought in some breakfast from the rucksack. I zipped my opening closed again, writhed out of the warm nightwear and rolled up the sleeping bag. Then lay a minute or two. Like a dragonfly from the chrysalis, it's the moment of emergence when you're vulnerable. Quick out, dodging between the raindrops, and within 30 seconds I was a fully formed hillwalker, waterproof on the outside, fairly dry on the inside, and everything else in plastic bags in the sack.

A thorough soaking on Longside Edge is an enjoyable experience at any time. The glimpses of Derwentwater through the swirl, the flapping of the nylon jacket, the spray blowing off the puddles, the gleam of the wet rock. But best of all when you're heading down, not up, with a cosy car a thousand feet below.

From Bassenthwaite I looked back up Skiddaw and saw a rather high, very damp pile of stones. It didn't look like a top nightspot. But I knew better. In 15 hours on the hill (eight of them awake) I'd seen other people just once. On the other hand – despite thick mist, despite darkness – I'd seen an awful lot of Skiddaw.

2: BRUCE'S CROWN

Start/Finish:	Car parking at Caldons Campsite
Distance:	42 miles/68km
Ascent:	3900m/13,000ft
Approx. walking time:	24 hours
Terrain:	Grassy ridges, but rough forest rides and deep grass; five miles of forest road at the north end
Map:	Harvey's Galloway Hills is the only one to show the forest rides
Refreshments:	Shop at Caldons, cafe Stroan Bridge, House o' Hill Bargrennan
Public transport:	Buses to Glentrool Village

42 miles and 13,000ft of climb in 24 hours' walking time in the Galloway Hills on Britain's only long-distance bivvybag event.

The Route

A path follows Caldons Burn upstream to a fork at 270m/880ft altitude. Bear left to open slopes of Mulldonoch. From its low but rocky summit cross Lamachan Hill to Curlywee. Descend southeast for 200 yards, then south to a plateau where a wall leads down to Loup of Laggan. Head down right, on boggy path, to a convenient point to strike up to Drigmorn Hill. Cross Millfore to Cairngarroch and descend very deep grass to the forest road below. Cross the bridge over the Black Water (first checkpoint).

Climb to left of a quarry (small path) onto an open hill. Cross Darrou and Little Millyea to Meikle Millyea. The superb Rhinns of Kells ridge runs north over Corserine and Carlin's Cairn to Coran of Portmark. Return towards Bow and choose a tree gap to head down to a forest road alongside Loch Doon. This descent is arduous. Turn left to the bridge of Gala Lane (second checkpoint; supper stop; optional bivvy stop).

A forest road leads to a junction south of Ballochbeatties. Turn right for 400 yards to a ride that leads up onto Shiel Hill. From this cross

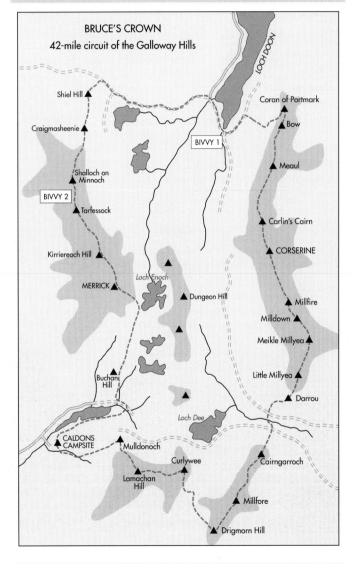

BRUCE'S CROWN
42-mile circuit of the Galloway Hills

LOCH DOON

Shiel Hill

Coran of Portmark

Bow

Craigmasheenie

Meaul

BIVVY 1

Shalloch on Minnoch

BIVVY 2

Tarfessock

Carlin's Cairn

CORSERINE

Kirriereoch Hill

Loch Enoch

MERRICK

Dungeon Hill

Millfire

Milldown

Meikle Millyea

Little Millyea

Darrou

Buchan Hill

Loch Dee

CALDONS CAMPSITE

Mulldonoch

Curlywee

Cairngarroch

Lamachan Hill

Millfore

Drigmorn Hill

rough rocky ground over Craigmasheenie, then grass over Shalloch on Minnoch to the following col (Nick of Carclach) which has water and small lochans (checkpoint; second optional bivvy stop).

Small ridge-path leads onwards to a steep stony ascent of Kirriereoch, then a sharp ridge onto Merrick. The event route now descends to the southwest corner of Loch Enoch and runs along the ridge to Buchan Hill. Descend with care (small crags) to the stile at Buchan. A track leads left, to a path and footbridge above the head of Loch Trool. A well-built path along the loch's north shore leads back to Caldons.

After the first five hours, the fast people are out of sight in front and the slow ones are out of sight behind – if, that is, they haven't already retired, once they hit the thigh-high squashy grass coming down off Cairngarroch. So the ones you overtake are the inexperienced who started too fast. For them, the engrossing struggle with exhaustion and self-doubt starts here, at the climb onto the Kells range, barely 10 miles into the event.

Bruce's Crown: running to Curleywee

But even here, overtaking is a slow and sociable process, stretching over several hills. And once we reach the long grassy crest, with the rocky crags eastwards where the goats lurk and the view west to the grey granite and the silver lochans, we all seem to forget that thigh-high tussocky bit, the grim struggle with the bracken on Darrou. After nine miles of goatlike gambolling along the high Rhinns of Kells comes the plunge through the forest down to Loch Doon, where even Harvey's fling up their theodolite and say you're on your own, mate. The descent is a complex game of chance, akin to pinball. Drop in a whole load of walkers and runners at the top; shake them up thoroughly; and they all pop out at the bottom in a completely different order.

At the bottom we jog the track, pineneedles gradually working their way down and dropping out of our trouser bottoms, to the first of Glyn's tricks of clockwork.

The rules of the event have, over the years, become positively theological, as organiser Glyn Jones tries to arrange salvation for all entrants from top hillrunners to the slow but serious. This is the first of two bedrooms. If you arrive after 5pm, you *may* turn off your stopwatch and stay the night. If you arrive after 8pm, you *must* stay for the night. While we who arrive at 4pm *are not allowed* to go to bed yet, but have up to 30 minutes' free time in which to eat the nectarines and homemade fruitcake. This means we have the chance to make the acquaintance of runners from just in front and just behind, even as the Doonside midges make their acquaintance with us.

Five miles of flat forest road is a challenge of a different sort, to be run while digesting nectarines in the fading light. And then we made a mess of it through the pine prickles, ending up coming downhill onto a side-ride to meet two runners from 10 minutes ahead coming up – yes, they'd even more of a mess of it than us. And then a surprise bite in the ankle from Galloway: the two small hills of Shiel and Craigmasheenie, grey rock and deep orange grass. Lose a shoe in the moss at this time of night and you'll still be looking for it when the sun comes up.

But first, the sun has to go down. This it does behind the Isle of Arran, as we stand and admire it from Shalloch on Minnoch. We had to stop and stand anyway – there's a control punch at the top of Shalloch. The black Isle of Arran floated in a fluorescent orange sea that exactly matched the plastic control punch my cold fingers fumbled for.

This is a low-budget, low-impact event. The controls are marked with squares cut from a chunky red milk crate. This item too is colour co-ordinated with the Atlantic sunset.

Seven in the evening and here's the second optional dormitory. Under the rules, we *aren't obliged* to stop, but *may* if we want. And the light is fading. The third dormitory, supposing we found it in the dark, would leave only 10 miles for tomorrow; and the ridge of Tarfessock is, anyway, utterly uninviting. While here at Bedroom Two there's a huge comfy boulder of erratic granite to lean against; best Galloway tussocks to lie down on; a lochan reflecting the fading of the day; and a dozen tired and happy hillrunners for social intercourse.

If you pass the second and also the third dormitory before 8pm, you can complete the whole thing in one, and it is only 42 miles, so why not? Two entrants confident in their ability to do just that had equipped themselves with just plastic bivvybags. Two entrants are now settling down at Bedroom Two for an uncomfortable plastic night.

Bruce's Crown: bivvy on Tarfessock

Galloway tussocks are excellent insulation, but the reason why sleep was quite so deep and cosy is revealed when I draw back the green plastic at dawn. A warm blanket of cloud has pulled itself over the heather bed, and it's drizzling.

I set out before it was quite light, hoping to finish within 24 hours overall. Starting in the dark is nonsense in terms of net competitive time, but good sense in the matter of blood-red sunrises, of early mists pooling above Loch Enoch. And down in the Galloway heartland, the people on the short route have trampled a nice path around the silvery lochans, through the heather and the swamps.

The short route? It's half the length of the full circuit, over ground that's twice as tough. Thirty-one of the 70 starters found that they could satisfy their appetite for granite moorland, silver-sanded beaches and heather bog without needing to consume all of the 20 miles and 1800m/6000ft offered. Our route around the grassy perimeter has been higher but less intensely Galloway.

And so along the final grassy, rocky ridge and the new smooth path at the back of Loch Trool. With runners and walkers arriving at every hour of the 24, the finish meal is a combination breakfast/lunch/supper lasting all day. Hungry runners feed on fruitcake and tinned rice pudding, while hungry midges feed on runners.

Because of the complicated time-allowances, nobody knows who's 'won', but one man did squeeze past the third bivvy-point before the eight o'clock bedtime, to subject himself to the very special experience of Galloway heartland in the dark – thus spoiling his chance of a prizewinning time, except that Glyn had that in mind all along so there's a prize anyway for just this achievement.

Results? It depends what you mean by results. I didn't know whether I came 7th or 17th. I do know I had 42 miles of great Galloway running on Britain's only bivvybag endurance event. It's been happening every two years since 1990, and the entry address is at the back of the book.

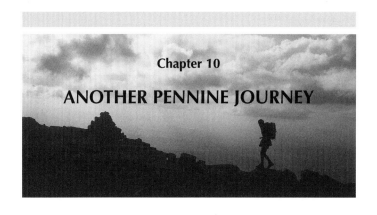

Chapter 10

ANOTHER PENNINE JOURNEY

RE-ENACTING WAINWRIGHT ON A WALK TO THE ROMAN WALL

'The way also here was very wearisome through dirt and slabbiness: nor was there on all this ground so much as one inn or victualling-house wherein to refresh the feebler sort.'

John Bunyan, *Pilgrim's Progress*

Total distance:	205 miles/330km (of which 18 miles on road, 38 miles shared with Pennine Way)
Total ascent:	8600m/29,000ft
Terrain:	Mostly clear and followable paths, some open hill, some invisible field paths requiring navigation
Maps:	1:25,000 Outdoor Leisure are best for finding paths; 30, 31, 43, 19 cover most of the route. Landrangers 98 and 87 fill the gaps.
Best bar meals:	Tan Hill Inn; Royal Oak, Appleby; Sun Inn, Dent
Best takeaway:	Fish & chips, Haltwhistle; filled rolls from Alston bakery

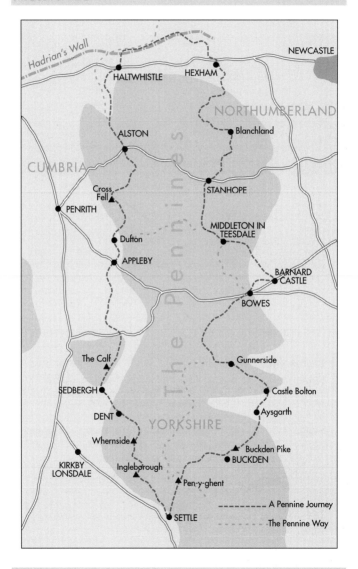

In September of 1938 Alfred Wainwright took a fortnight off from the Town Hall at Bolton and went for a walk. In September of 1998 I took off after him, to see what 60 years had done to the Pennines, to the paths of the Pennines and to the people who walk on those paths.

Wainwright's route-plan was simple. He got off the train at Settle, and walked up the east side of the Pennines to the Roman Wall. He walked along the wall, and then he walked back down the west side to Settle. I would follow Wainwright's route-plan; but not Wainwright's route. In 1938 the easy way from dale to dale was the road. The road was lightly tarred, if tarred at all, and a car passed every half-hour. In 1998 the car ruled the road – but the rest of the map was covered all over with pink dots and dashes. And in 1998 we could be confident that those pink dots would lead, on the ground, to stiles and even signposts. And if today's off-roads are longer and more complicated than Wainwright's on-roads, the effect is merely to make the Pennines bigger. And why should we complain of that?

I left Wainwright in Ribblesdale and headed up onto Pen-y-ghent. Gradually, that splendid south ridge undissolved out of the haze, appearing ahead and also overhead. The steps in it, which give it its exhilarating shape, are caused by the Yoredale Series of rocks: hard limestone, hard gritstone and soft shale, layered like sandwiches squashed together after several million years in the bottom of the rucksack.

Wainwright really enjoyed his northward journey up the east: crossing each moor, looking suddenly down into each new valley, getting ever closer to the wall. For me, though, the moor crossings were investigations of the grey, with nothing to see but peat.

Still, one can't be grey all day. Take Aysgarth, where a bootscraper outside the church makes it easy for you to wander into the cool and enjoy the limestone altar screen and the fresh chrysanths, the cool air and the space – more cool and air in Aysgarth Church than up on Whitaside Moor, in fact. Then at the falls they've made new paths that let you enjoy the water from various directions while still linking in to the pink dots of the right-of-way. At Swaledale I searched out the miners' path that wanders below outcrops, above outcrops, on a grassy shelf high above the Swale Gorge. I saw the lights of Tan Hill from far

Upper Swaledale

across the moor, and heard its friendly generator rumble across the bog.

My days fell into a pattern. I switched on the torch at five or half-past, changed into cooler clothes and rolled up the bivvybag. I set off at six, to snatch a half-hour from the pre-dawn, and got lost at six-fifteen. I got lost (later) in Dentdale, I got lost and almost wandered into a quarry at Westgate, I got lost on the golf course at Hexham. But the first and finest of the losts was at Tan Hill, where I wandered in the dark, knee-deep in peat and heather, looking for the Pennine Way on Bowes Moor. (I found it in the end: they'd moved it across the Sleightholme Beck for drier ground.)

Walks need hills like cake needs flour – but a walk that's all hill isn't cake, it's bread. The wooded riverbanks were another of the good bits. First there was the little Deepdale Beck. Its wood has gritty outcrops and blackberries (plus, of course, the thorns that go with the blackberries).

Then there was a big river: the Tees. Right away you get the walk's second-best footbridge. It's a great arch of iron, and the gaps in the planks show a long drop to a deep pool, while just downstream is the castle bit of Barnard Castle looking all threatening and Border Country.

I walked up the Tees for five hours; during that time, there got to be a lot less Tees. It was still a river, but a merrier one – not averse to a bit of teenage giggling when it got to a rocky bit, and some childish leaping around. And Teesdale had got smaller too. The moors were only a field or two above, and there was an upland chill in the air.

The Pennine Way had only just started its Tees bit, and headed off into the central moorlands with a wave: 'See you on the way back!'

While Wear wasn't actually wearisome, the crossing into it was the least exciting of them all. Pathless grass (not pathless bog: there was still limestone under the moors) led up into the mist. I looked at my compass, and not much else, and reached a road pass with a cattle-grid. Tees/Wear footpaths are widely spaced, and for once I was going to sink morally (climb physically) onto a high-level moorland road.

There was a single point of interest. Wainwright here took a short-cut, a vile muddy trod cutting an angle of the descent, before regaining with relief the 'green road'. The road in 1998 was tarmac-grey – but the vile trod was still there on the 1:50,000 map. As I'd expected, it has become a grassy trundle, with a few cartwheel grooves to show where Wainwright wallowed in long-gone days before the war.

I dropped out of mist into darkness, crossed the bottom of Weardale by streetlight, and got up onto a grassy moor. In the morning I dropped to Rookhope, and got up onto a heathery moor. Hexhamshire Common, it's called: 10 miles of heather in every direction, criss-crossed by tracks of ancient lead-miners and modern gunners-down of grouse.

Even the map shows little hereabouts: some brown contour rings, placenames marking no particular places: 'Ladle Well', a hut; 'Broad Mere', a hillside; 'Stobb Cross', a track junction; 'Hangman Hill', another track junction. If you can't see the country then enjoy the map. Consider Hangman Hill – hangings took place, like modern tourist information centres, in town centres, and if this was anything it was the site of a gibbet, where the resulting corpses would be hung in chains as awful warnings. (Nowadays, they'd be using the green bits in the middles of roundabouts.)

Hexham, on a damp autumn Sunday, is the same blackish-brown all over. The old parts of the town lean tiredly against each other so as not to fall over. Some of them have sunk below street level, and have boards across the doorways to stop the Tyne getting in when it floods.

Hexham's main heritage feature is an interesting prison. It'd be a real pity to visit Hexham on a sunny day – sunshine would spoil the atmosphere completely.

The wall, wanting you to get the full accumulated impact, unfolds itself very, very gradually. For a hundred miles of the walk it's an idea merely, and at the first car park, at Milecastle 31, it's little more. There's an interpretation board, a path with a bull on it, and a hump that used to be a Mithraeum until they took the Mithraeum away to a museum.

After that there's the Vallum. Vallum, second declension, neuter, 'a rampart', if you went to that sort of school. The rampart is a grass one, built before the wall and running alongside it. It's up out of the bog, and lovely brisk walking. The wall itself was torn down to make the military road, and the modern road lies on top of it. General Wade, that was; cultural vandalism excused by military necessity. The same military necessity, of course, that led to the wall in the first place – keeping out the Scots. Wade was stuck at Newcastle as Bonnie Prince Charlie invaded by Carlisle, and didn't want to get caught the same way again.

The next interpretation board has real stonework, and a sharp ridge rises ahead. In Sewingshields Wood, the edge of the trees is the edge of everything: I looked out between the trunks to miles of empty moor – empty but for the imaginary Picts and barbarians lurking in the dead ground. At the wood's end I stepped over a stile and there it was. Six feet of ancient stonework, the built line following the line of the ridge in curves and dips right into the distance, and on the Scottish side the sudden drop of the Whinstone Sill. I went back into the wood and had a sandwich, just so as to step over that stile a second time.

For those 15 miles it marches the grassy brink of the whinstone, looking out across the grey-green billows of the empty north, so that it's like a cliff walk. Like a cliff walk too in the way it keeps on going down and round a little bend and up again. But at the same time it's a cliff walk with history. You can't help thinking of the legionaries who built it, and proudly carved their name and regiment at the end of every section. You can't help thinking of the men who manned it: half-barbarian auxiliaries, mostly, from Romania and the Balkans. With what suspicion they must have looked out at this cold and alien landscape, inhabited by surly locals who were barbarians too, but of a quite different sort of barbarity. And yet we know that they came to love this bleak land, for when their service was finished they retired here, and carved out farmsteads, and sent their sons to stand on the milecastle turrets and gaze north into the dangerous wild lands.

In 1938 Wainwright turned south from the wall with real sadness, and from this point on his book becomes quite dismal. There's a point on any walk – whether it's 10 miles or a couple of thousand – where the end is in sight but not yet in reach, and where it's rather easy to lose your sense of fun. You can detect it, I think, in Hamish Brown's Groats End Walk. After 1500-odd miles he hits Ireland, with Wales and the South West still before him; and somehow, though five days ahead of himself, suddenly feels he has to press on, and avoids all the small hills he'd planned, and walks the roads between his 13 Irish Three-thousands. And it happened here to Wainwright. After six days' walking

Cautley Crag in the Howgills

towards the Wall he found himself with nothing before him but six days' walking back again. He walked the road for a day, and then the weather turned nasty on him so he walked the road for another day, and ended up walking the road all the way to Settle.

The way to avoid this low point is to throw in some high ground. Cross Fell, the Howgills, and the remaining two of the Yorkshire Three

Peaks were my plan to keep my walking – and hence, I hoped, my spirits – up.

South Tyne is a lovely valley. Wainwright liked it even, walking despondent along what is now the A689. I enjoyed it more by wood and footbridge, and came as the day faded onto the line of an empty railway. That evening, and on the following day, I was to walk the South Tyne for eight hours. And yet I never felt, as in Teesdale I did feel, that I might eventually tire of Tyne. Each bend of the river brings a new bit of valley, all different, but all in tones of gentle green. My journey, from the pretty to the grim, was already turning back towards the pretty.

At dusk, then, I veered up from the river and found the railway line, and walked out from under trees into a high bright place. Stand on Lambley viaduct in the last light. See the river gleam, the valley winding into darkness, and the light of a single farm and of a car two miles away. It was so quiet I heard the river murmuring on its pebbles a hundred feet below. That, of course, was the one footbridge finer than the aqueduct at Barnard Castle.

Wainwright suffered, on the stormy road pass a thousand feet below, looking across at Lakeland. But on Cross Fell's top, in cool autumn with the bog-grass fading orange and sunlight not too far away, you can look at Blencathra and not mind too much. Anyway, Blencathra's in the cloud.

The Pennines, east to west, resemble the FTSE Index: they creep up slowly, a bit at a time, but the drop when it comes is sudden and surprising. The main rivers flow out to the North Sea, and on the northward journey I'd crossed them one by one: Ure and Swale, Wharfe and Tees and Wear. Coming south in the west, though, the Pennines are one long edge, dropping to the plains as suddenly as, on the day I stood on that edge looking at Lakeland, the FTSE was dropping due to the collapse of something called a hedge fund in America.

The Vale of Eden is the one low moment in the high-level southward romp. The banks of a stream (the Hoff Beck) give walking that's less intellectually demanding than stile to stile, and easier on the eye. The stream seems a small one, considering that, three miles upstream, it's due to erupt into a waterfall recommended by the Tourist Board as one of the wonders of Westmorland. There is a cafe alongside it which, sadly, is not open at 8am. The fall itself is a wide white fan dropping into a duck pond.

In map terms the Howgills come between the Pennines and the Lakes; but in mountain terms they're somewhere else altogether. The Lakes are volcanic rocks, with knobs. The Pennines are wide flat grit, with stirrings of peculiar limestone. The Howgills are soft shale, carved into deep steep valleys and coated in velvety grass. Consider the lines of a fell pony: the elegant curve of the creature, the smooth strokable coat, the intelligent eye. The Howgills are fell pony country.

I strode up a long rounded ridge onto the Howgills. The day was hazy, but the haze had drizzle in it. Cloud brushed the summits, and a brisk invigorating wind. As I got higher the wind got brisker, till I started to fear for the security of my woolly hat. The sides of Kensgriff are grass that's steep – steep as Lakeland rock, almost – for the wind to rush up the side, a quick eddy at the top, and down again into a long lonely valley. Flat shadows on the left, across Rawthey, were glimpses of the Pennines, but more interesting by far were the tall cones of Howgill, fading bump behind bump into the grey.

In Sedbergh it was raining stair-rods, and night was falling early into the narrow, stone-sided streets. Yellow shop lights sparkled on wet cobbles.

Wainwright was very struck by Dent. A grim hole, he calls it, where mean hovels crowd so close that even the bus has to stop outside the village. And where the bus cannot penetrate, what chance for other appurtenances of civilisation?

Dent, today, has those same mean hovels lovingly preserved, the same grey cobbled streets. That said, the cobble turns back to proper tarmac right at the 30-mile limit, and the effect is altogether unconvincing. The cobbles are too clean, and Dent's twin pubs too homely and convivial. Only the public toilets, where I changed into dry things for the pub, preserve a whiff of former sordid Dent.

On the wide north ridge of Whernside, on a misty day, there's nothing to see but grass. The grass moves around in the wind, and the wind flaps in your jacket and stops you thinking – not that there's much to think about, when you're on the seventh day and the 170th mile, and you haven't quite got around to waking up yet, and there's 600m/2000ft to climb on wide grass. Even the compass bearing – due south – isn't all that interesting.

After a while I heard a strange beating noise, like a badly pitched tent in the wind. I turned – or thought I turned – and saw Alfred

Wainwright walking just beside me. His cycle cape was flapping out in front, and the rain was streaming down his spectacles, and he was breathing through his teeth and grinning.

Despite the bootnails coming through into his foot and the encumbrance of the cycle cape, he didn't seem to be having any trouble keeping up. The wind was too strong for conversation.

A corner of water appeared among the grass stalks. I had found the Whernside Tarns. (I expect Wainwright, who never carried a compass, was quite impressed with my navigation.) The Tarns could have been any size, but the waves coming down out of the mist and splashing among the tussocks suggested quite big. The map, on the other hand, suggests quite small. After the tarns the ridge goes hummocky, but it was easy to keep direction – whenever I turned aside the wind blew my hood off. Wainwright's cape, meanwhile, was up around his ears.

I considered swapping him – faded Gore-tex clone for cycle cape. He'd have to get the hang of the zips, of course, while I could still remember toggles from my boyhood days in tents with wooden poles.

Wainwright was no softie. Wainwright, indeed, was a bivouacker – he warmly commends Hollow Stones, under Scafell, as a place to spend an informal night out. And Wainwright had had as good a time as a person can have, in a hopeless cycle cape in a storm, walking flooded roads under two feet of water. How thrilled he was going to be with a waterproof that really does keep out most of the water, a hood that really doesn't let wet trickles down the neck, and zips that work with cold fingers!

We're neither of us enthusiastic shoppers. My hill jacket is more of a cheap fashion item, and neither as waterproof nor as breathable as it had been a thousand miles back in its history. All the same, it is a garment designed by a thoughtful and ingenious person for having fun in storms in.

Perhaps, in my jacket, Wainwright would have taken hills not roads, and enjoyed the return half of his Pennine journey. Perhaps he would have gone home pleased with the Pennines, and discovered, on arrival, that the fair maid and muse of his hilltop longings, and his wife Betty, were one and the same. And the seven Wainwright Guides would be guides to the Yorkshire Three Peaks, and we'd still be calling Blencathra Saddleback. Lakeland walkers, lacking Alfred, would have to follow Harry Griffin. And so, today, we'd all be scrambling in the Great End

Ingleborough from Whernside

gullies, and ski-ing the ridges of Helvellyn, and doing Red Screes from the Kirkstone as quickly as possible…

The summit wall appeared out of the mist. The map said there was a big path on the other side, and there was. Beyond the path was a drop, and the wind coming up out of it was the wind from the Howgills. It was wind with plenty of rain in, coming sideways in gusts and buffets, and it wasn't at all easy to stay on the path, wide as it was.

I was jolly glad I hadn't let Wainwright have my jacket.

You walk with someone for half a day, feel you're starting to know them – and then they stop to take something out of the sack and are gone forever. Wainwright was sitting dripping in some inn, six foot tall in a torn cycle cape, wondering if those funny looks he was getting from the landlady's daughter meant that she fancied him.

Meanwhile I finished my own walk over Ingleborough and through 10 last lovely miles of limestone. And I thought about some other walker, 60 more years in the future, thinking about me and my walk. Will walkers in 2058, after two years' wait for the permit, join the queue along a Pennine Way that's tarred right up to Scotland? To preserve paths, walking may have to join the realm of simulated experience. In a sensory suit they'll tramp in the imagination, the more expensive machines having a treadmill to simulate authentic tiredness. There'll be a button to switch on the storm on Ingleborough, and, under strict medical supervision, a programme for imitation blisters.

Thinking about these things, and passing through the limestone, I realise that if there has ever been a golden age of walking it's now. We have the gear we need – almost-breathable near-waterproof clothing, comfortable sacks, Compeed and Moleskin for the feet, and lightweight boots. We have – and it's only in the last 10 years that we've really had it – the right-of-way network, and a usable path across every square mile of England. And we don't really have very many people walking at our heels and telling us what we mustn't do. The hills, it's true, are looking slightly trodden on. However, there's still plenty of room if you walk your own way, especially at a silly time of year. In September 1938, Wainwright met two other hikers. In 1998, I met six long-distance walkers: four on the Pennine Way and two on the soon-to-be Hadrian's Trail. I met some soldiers, a man on Cross Fell, and a large party coming down off the moors of the upper Tees.

It's still a big enough place, England.

ROUTE DETAILS

The route stays off-road wherever possible and takes the most direct-looking right-of-way. From Settle, it follows the Ribble to Stainforth, then crosses Pen-y-ghent to Foxup. Climb Horse Head Moor and follow the Wharfe to Buckden for Buckden Pike. Walden Beck leads to Aysgarth.

Pass Aysgarth Falls to Castle Bolton, and head up Apedale to reach Gunnerside and Ivelet. High on the north side of the Swale Gorge, a little-used path runs to Swinner Gill and Keld. Follow the Pennine Way to Bowes.

Paths through Deepdale wood run down to Barnard Castle. Cross the Tees and head upstream, recrossing to stay on paths, to Bowlees. A bridleway leads to Scar End for an undefined path to the road pass at Swinhope Head. Join the Weardale Way at Westgate and head northeast to Rookhope.

Cross the moors to Ramshaw and Baybridge. Tracks lead west to Hangman Hill. Take the Long Drag (track beside Linn Burn) then field paths to Juniper. More paths lead north into Hexham.

Follow the Tyne to West Boat, then circle north of Fourstones to reach the line of Hadrian's Wall just east of Milecastle 31. A path (not right-of-way) follows the Vallum to left of the B6318 until the wall heads off to the right. Follow the wall to Great Chesters, where a streamside path leads down to Haltwhistle.

Follow paths alongside the South Tyne to Slaggyford and join the Pennine Way. This leads through Alston and Garrigill onto Cross Fell and then down to Dufton (nice diversion to left of Dufton Pike). Paths lead via Flakebridge to Appleby.

Head southwest to join Hoff Beck, which is followed most of the way to Great Asby. Cross Asby Scar to Sunbiggin Tarn and take a rough path to Brownber. Cross Randygill Top, Yarlside and Great Dummacks to Sedbergh.

A path across Frostrow Fells leads to Dentdale. Head up from Whernside Manor onto Whernside, then cross Ingleborough. Descend past Gaping Gill to Wharfe and Feizor for a delightful finish along Giggleswick Scar.

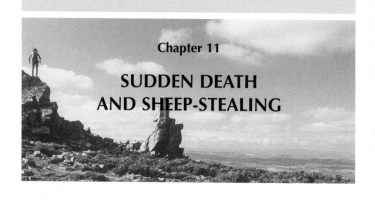

Chapter 11

SUDDEN DEATH AND SHEEP-STEALING

A CROSSING OF PUMLUMON FAWR

Start:	Church Stretton, Shropshire
Finish:	Aberystwyth
Distance:	84 miles/135km
Total ascent:	3600m/12,000ft
Terrain:	Paths, fields and grassy hilltops
Access:	Rights-of-way, and open hill on Pumlumon Fawr
Maps:	Landrangers 137, 126, 125, 136, 135
Public transport:	Railway stations at start and finish; connection is via Shrewsbury
Accommodation:	Church Stretton, Bridges, Stiperstones Village, Hopesgate, Marton, Lower Leighton, Welshpool, Llanfair, Cefn Coch, Carno, Dylife, Tal-y-bont, Borth, Aberystwyth

Right in the middle of Wales, between the Christmas trees and the reservoirs, there stands a green, gently sloping hill that just manages to reach the 760m/2500ft contour. It's got a sort of English/Welsh name, and it's a sort of English/Welsh hill that would be quite at home in the Pennines. You start from a convenient car park, and go up over yellow grass and rushes. The path is boggy, but not challengingly boggy. The wind stirs the cloud like a listless catering operative making soup on National Minimum Wage. Soon after leaving the car you reach a clump of cairns. Crouch behind them for a while. Chew on the sandwiches although you haven't really come far enough up to get properly hungry; plod down out of the mist, admire the view of Christmas trees, and wonder why you came.

That hill was called Plynlimon.

Also right in the middle of Wales is a real Welsh mountain with a real Welsh name: it's called Pumlumon Fawr. Pumlumon Fawr comes into Welsh poems involving sudden death and sheep stealing. Bones and broken weapons lie just below the turf. The Bronze Age raised its cairns here, and Glyndwr harried the English through the valley of Hengwm.

On the map, Plynlimon and Pumlumon Fawr seem to be two different names for a single summit. They're not. Plynlimon and Pumlumon Fawr are two different names for two quite different places. Once you've found Plynlimon, Pumlumon Fawr is round the back.

Sheep thieves and Welsh heroes always approach from a long way away. (They may not have much fun, but at least they get tired enough to appreciate the sandwiches.) They arrive at Pumlumon from Machynlleth, where Glyndwr had his parliament. Or they come in out of the green valleys of distant England.

I walked this in October, thinking a one-hill walk wouldn't be too demanding. But I needed all my mountain skills to navigate the unmarked rights-of-way of Montgomery – Plynlimon in the mist was to seem straightforward after that. Most of the paths are old, and a few have died and gone to heaven.

Such sufferings are worth pursuing in their own right; but as a bonus I discovered some unusual ground. Narrow craggy valleys are a linking feature of this walk; valleys where ravens wheel, where oaks twist black roots into yellow scree, where water falls and kestrels soar on the thermals. In a couple of these small hollows you can add a touch of real fear to the loneliness, barbed wire, bewilderment and misery of the long wet winter nights.

The southern part of Shropshire is one of England's nicest non-mountain walking areas. 'Little Switzerland' is what they call the

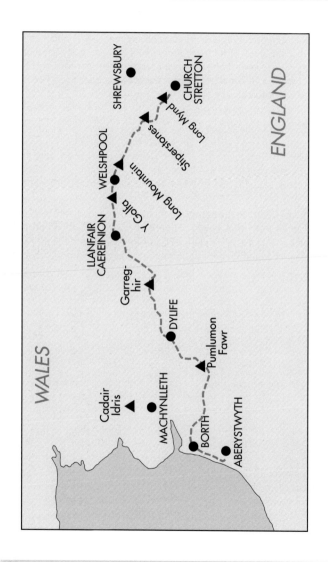

country around Church Stretton. The hills are small, but steep-sided and rocky-topped: Caer Caradoc and Stiperstones, Long Mynd and Lawley. In between is green country – green with pink dots, as Shropshire has a useful network of low-level rights-of-way. Those rights-of-way lead to small half-timbered towns, or thatched villages with pubs. If I have one complaint about prosperous Shropshire, it's that the thatch is all implausibly well repaired, and there's so much real ale that a pint of gassy nitrokeg is not to be had within a long day of walking. Even ordinary real ale may be hard to find as so many pubs brew their own really real ale in a shed at the back of the car park.

Ashes Hollow is the first of the rocky valleys: a bit of Pumlumon come raiding into England. Path and stream struggle for possession of the valley floor. Where there's not room for both, the path goes up for a little simple rock climbing onto the Long Mynd.

I bypassed the pub at Bridges as something better than beer was immediately above. The Stiperstones is a hill for lingering over. Quartzite rises in tors and silly pinnacles: every one of the delicious little outcrops may be scrambled over. One of them is the Devil's Chair, and under another lurks Wild Eldrick with his ghostly horde. But Glyndwr ahead will be far more frightening than English Eldrick, and I dozed in crimson bracken under autumn sun until rudely woken by a roar like flame bursting up over the hill.

The strange sound was, in fact, merely flame bursting up over the hill. A hot-air balloon was burning propane immediately overhead, so as not to crash its basket into the Devil's Chair. I watched it float off over Shropshire, then headed Wales-ward down a grassy hollow.

I left Stiperstones village on what the map calls 'road used as public path' to Venus Bank. Actually it's 'road not used as anything at all', but I found where it wasn't once my compass had suggested where to look.

Long Mountain may not be much of a mountain, but it is quite long. I got well scratched looking for its trig point, which is in the middle of a thicket. Here I met the Welsh Border and Offa's Dyke Path. Offa certainly seemed to be enjoying itself along the length of Long Mountain, with a sudden view down into the Severn valley.

In Welshpool there was good Greek pizza. For dessert I enjoyed the delicious pink confection of Powys Castle, half a mile out of town. And two miles out of town, on the Welsh side, is a small hill called Y Golfa.

Four miles out of town, on the English side, is another small hill called Y Golfa. Is this international one-upmanship, or are the two nations trying to confuse each other? The Welsh one has a golf course. Either 'Golfa' is the Welsh for golf course or it's Welsh for something else such as 'sharp pointy place where we ambushed the English' and some clever golf course impresario persuaded a non-linguistic planning officer he didn't need planning permission...

Y Golfa is small but thorny. I bedded down under the prickles, and at dawn walked along its southern edge, my eyes following the sliced golfballs down into the valley below. That valley is called Einion; it's pronounced like the root vegetable but is considerably tastier with its little green hills and hanging woodland. But oh, its rights-of-way are tricky: up the little hill, down through the wood, and back across the river. And in behind Cefn Coch I was offered two propositions: that rights-of-way weren't intended for the likes of me, and that the friendly-looking wolfhound was going to tear me to bits. I was escorted through. Others may prefer the road.

On the Stiperstones, looking west across Wales

By mid-morning I was out of this difficult country and up on the moors of Cefn-gwyn. This is fast, flat and open: eyes wander for miles while stomach settles after the bouncing around the Einion valley.

Garreg-hir is a proper little mountain: rock emerges from the grassland and crinkles itself into nooks for eating lunch in. And then the grassland curves suddenly, and there at my feet is the Pennant valley with its farms and little stream, and a steep nasty drop to get down into it by.

Pumlumon Fawr is a real mountain, and real mountains have rocky bits. However, the rocky mountainous bits of Pumlumon are like those sheep of the heroic age: they're never where they're meant to be; instead you'll find them 15 miles away in someone else's valley. And this deep hollow of Pennant could be the high point of the whole walk.

Above the Afon Twymyn are orange bracken and grey boulders; and above the bracken the woods tip sideways and rise straight into the sky. I almost expect avalanche debris and a lonely goatherd singing choruses from *The Sound of Music*. Some fierce sculptures have been constructed out of locally available materials – dead trees, cow dung and bindertwine. Seen in fading light, the wolf man looks pretty horrible; and so does the slope behind him which I have to climb.

But the wolf man doesn't bite, and the path ascends in gentle green zigzags. There's a waterfall, there are ravens, and there are only 200m/700ft of ascent. At the top take a breath, cross a stile, and emerge to high pastures and the Star Inn at Dylife. The landscape up here is dead, and dead by violence. Its dreary heather cannot cover the scars and slash-marks of old mines.

I hurried on to the moorland above, which was merely sheep-nibbled and treeless.

The gorge of Afon Clywedog is probably a lot less impressive than Pennant – but I was doing it in the mist, in the dark. On the left the rushes and tussocks dropped away sharply, and the splash and roar coming up out of the pit of darkness made the Afon Clywedog sound really deep and exciting. My torch found a tiny crag, with deep rushes at its foot, so I stopped and used the roar of the gorge as a lullaby.

With the coast and civilisation now a mere mountain away, I rose early. In clouded half-light, tracks of mud and gravel took me into the hill for miles and miles. Not all lakes are jewel-like; the tracks took me past two that are grey and cheerless like the tarnished armour of the English who never made it back to Shrewsbury. And then it dropped me off at the end of a long hole full of tussocks.

Now I was really beginning to enter the Pumlumon experience.

I struggled with the tussocks for a while, just to get the feel of them. I climbed slowly, damply, onto the ridge. It's not a crest, or an arête, or anything like that. It's wide and flat, with a fence and some peatpools. The grass is short and easy to go on. I was enjoying it because it wasn't the tussocks, but at the same time I started to get a little nervous. For miles and miles in every direction, there was nowhere that was anywhere at all. Thirty miles away in the southwest I could make out the orange glow of a place where streetlights were shining dimly onto wet early-morning streets.

This is the middle of Wales, which is as close to the middle of Nowhere as you'll get in these British Isles.

The slope on the right steepened, actually grew a few rocks and an edge I could fall over. And suddenly, grey lumps in the mist were Pumlumon's cairns; a cairn from the Bronze Age and a cairn from the Hillwalking Age and a middle-period trig point.

I trotted merrily down to Y Garn and crossed the dam of Nant-y-moch. It's a great grim reservoir that crawls away into the hills like a dragon with bad pneumonia.

Next comes some black bewildering woodland: except that October is just after the Long Distance Walkers' Association have walked across Wales. Their friendly footprints, and odd scraps of pink tape tied to the twigs, kept me company through the trees. The LDWA come out of England over Plynlimon to the sea – but they do it from Anchor, so it's only 45 miles. On the other hand, they do it in a single day...

Their scuffmarks lead out of the wood, across a field, and past a grey tarn with drizzle falling into it. And then the path leaps suddenly into a rocky hollow that, if Pennant wasn't already nominated, would be the deep-down high point of the walk.

The bottom of Craig y Pistyll is a leaping stream and the sides are scree. Damp bracken and crags rise above. The path is narrow and loose. Below it, the screes drop a few metres and then disappear over a cliff; you have to be careful not to do the same thing yourself.

I reached the valley bottom all too soon. Ahead was a small hill – small enough to be below the cloud and so let me see the sea, just five miles ahead.

Cors Fochno is a Raised Mire of International Importance. As I was walking at sea-level and the Raised Mire of International Importance is – well – raised, I saw only its first few brambles. The view was like what I'd seen from the top of Pumlumon Fawr: grey nothingness with wind in. But this wind was warmer and smelled of salt. And so I came across watermeadows into the back of Borth.

Actually, Borth is all back. Wearing faded lipstick and a sunhat with holes in, Borth peers across the Irish Sea hoping to glimpse the other side, and meanwhile scratches a living by selling itself beachballs.

I walk south along the sand-scoured esplanade, grey sea on the right, faded hotels on the left. At the end of the front was a cliff path all the way to Aberystwyth. The path is signed and waymarked: the tired brain can take a rest, the battered map can be folded and put away, leaving hands free for the ham roll of Borth. Down at sea-level the waves crash around in the usual way: it's a cracking cliff path.

Constitution Hill gives a sudden view of Aberystwyth, and an even more sudden drop to the end of its waterfront. Along the waterfront elderly ladies in wheelchairs, well wrapped, are being pushed by smart young ones. The hotels are less faded here than at Borth, but even bigger. The fake-Georgian lamp posts are actually genuine Georgian.

Walk's end is a monument depicting the Spirit of Sunbathing. Out to sea point her bronzed nipples: inland, her sunburnt bum. Above hovers a winged figure representing the ozone layer.

This walk started at Little Switzerland, and here it finishes at a seedy seaside resort that's not quite Nice. Taken from end to end, it hasn't quite been the famous GR5 from Geneva to the Mediterranean.

Hundreds of high Alpine mountains weren't crossed, just one rather low one in Wales. No goats gambolled over the flower-decked pastures, just bad-tempered sheepdogs. Spicy red-hot gluwein wasn't served on checked tablecloths: here you get pizza and chips in Welshpool, and a bivvy under a thorntree. This is a very English-and-Welsh walk.

Autumn and spring bring their days of golden sunshine. Cosy valleys and small rocky places; bright berries and turning leaves; moonlight over grey moors. These are the walk from Switzerland to Aberystwyth – from Shropshire to the Sea.

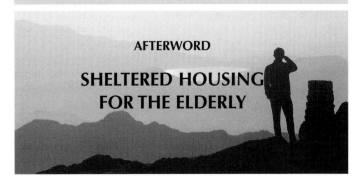

AFTERWORD

SHELTERED HOUSING FOR THE ELDERLY

Once there was a man called Ivan Waller. In 1931 he climbed behind Colin Kirkus on a seriously overhanging route called Mickledore Grooves in the days when falling off generally meant death, or severe injury if you were really lucky.

What happens to mountaineers as they get older? They just turn into older mountaineers. At the age of 70 Ivan turned to the Munros and climbed 140 of them in two years to become Munroist number 207. Three years later he backpacked across Scotland in the Ultimate Challenge event.

Still in his seventies he completed the 45-mile walk of the Lakeland 914m/3000ft peaks in a day, and climbed Tower Ridge in winter conditions without causing the slightest anxiety to my cousin, who was his companion. He also traversed the Cuillin Ridge twice, the second time escorting an older companion.

He considered the Corbetts: 'This may be beyond my span because I still have more than 160 to do at 81 years of age, but a man can always try.' However, there might be some mileage in the 'Metros' – those hills that would have been Munros if Sir Hugh had started counting at 900m instead of the slightly higher 3000ft. This idea gathers in an extra 27 mountains, quite a few of which are really rather good ones. There is steep-sided Streap, above Glenfinnan; there is Sgurr Cos na Breachd-laoigh, rough and rocky at the heart of Knoydart. There are also quite a few which really aren't rather good at all. One such is Beinn Bhreac, in the forest of Atholl.

The forest of Atholl has wide bogs, deep rivers and a lot of peat and heather. Beinn Bhreac stands more or less in the middle, slightly further from civilisation than Carn Ealar, which is considered the remotest of the existing Munros.

Ivan made an attack from a camp near Blair Atholl, but found his lightweight tent too heavy to carry through the peat hags. After further attempts by bicycle from Glen Feshie and Glen Tilt, he learnt about the benefits of the Gore-tex bivvybag. For his fourth attempt he settled on the comparatively easy approach from Linn of Dee: a return journey of 32 miles.

By early evening he had reached the moorland ridge and was walking over rough gravel and grassland, lit by a savage sunset that beamed through the narrow gaps below a heavy cloud-layer at 900m/3000ft. At the lowest point of the ridge he passed a grassy corner below a little rock wall: a fairly inviting bivouac site.

The summit was reached at 8.30pm. Ivan's account is as follows:

'On the way back to the bivvy-site which I had spotted in the pass, the price was exacted for the stupendous sunset, when the whole northwestern sky turned black and torrential rain poured down. I hurried down to the pass and arrived with the outside of my Gore-tex garments streaming with water but beautifully dry inside. To have taken them off even for a moment would have seen me soaked to the skin in the deluge, but I had to get into my bivouac as it would soon be dark.

I spread out my mat which instantly collected pools of water, removed my boots, and stood temporarily in a plastic bag to keep my stockings dry. Luckily my down sleeping sacks were already arranged inside the Gore-tex bivvybag and I now had no alternative but to get straight into them, dripping outer garments and all. Miraculously my Polarfleece jacket kept my body warm, and the two layers of Gore-tex with the now thoroughly damp sleeping sacks between them kept me dry although I was lying in pools of water.

My feet were warm throughout the night, but for the first two hours before midnight the wind and rain continued and my legs began to chill so I organised some leg exercises. The bending and straightening were too much for my old sleeping sacks and there were feathers everywhere, all wet and matted.

By now I was beginning to ponder on the chances of an old man of 80 surviving this treatment, and then there was the worry about the effect of all this rain on the already swollen burn which would have to be crossed on the way home. Optimism was getting sorely strained but around midnight I fell asleep.

I woke up with the dawn, warm and comfortable soon after 4am and lay in for another hour. When I got up I found to my amazement that my bivvybag and my rucksack beside me were covered in an inch of snow. The clouds were down but the wind had dropped. Snow covered the ground but I was away in a few minutes.'

Later in life, Ivan took to smaller hills, seeking out those with silly or suggestive names: Great Cockup, Maiden's Paps. And when my cousin set out on his own crossing of Scotland, Ivan was there with planning and advice. There's no better way of walking eastwards than off Ben Nevis over all the Grey Corries. Into Atholl was the way to go, around the flanks of Beinn Bhreac.

My cousin wasn't quite certain about the three days of solo walking through the rough bounds of Knoydart, and invited me to accompany him for that bit. Ah, said Ivan, but if the weather's right you'll be wanting that bivvy on the Ciche. That's all right: the lad Ronald shall borrow my own bag.

Which is how I came to be sleeping in Ivan Waller's green Gore-tex on Sgurr na Ciche on a summer night of 1992.

MANUFACTURERS AND SUPPLIERS

All respectable mountain shops stock a range of bivvy bags. In case of difficulty, you can contact the manufacturers below. Web addresses tend to change, but they are mostly obvious (www.terra-nova.co.uk) or can be found by any search engine. Email addresses are on websites.

Terra Nova
Ecclesborne Park, Alfreton, Derbyshire DE55 4RF
Kathmandu Trekking seem to have rolled up their bag and vanished into the hills: the other source of inexpensive bivvy bags is military surplus, such as Surplus and Adventure Online, tel. 01386 793900 (currently stock Gore-tex bags at £60–£70) or Soldier of Fortune (mail-order) Unit 18 Tyn-y-Lidiart Industrial Estate, Corwen LL21 9RR, tel. 01490 412225

The British-made Outdoor Designs Alpine bivi (Gore-tex, about £100) and storm bivi (coated nylon, about £60) are available mail-order or online from **Cotswold Outdoor**, tel. 01666 575575 and the **Outdoor Shop**, tel. 01908 568913.

Bivvy bags are also made by **Mountain Hardwear, North Face, Outdoor Research, Mountain Range** and **Bibler**.

Materials (and patterns) for making your own, and for repairs:

Pennine Outdoor
2 Station Road, High Bentham, Lancaster LA2 7LF, tel. 015242 63377
Point North
Porthdafarch Road, Holyhead, Anglesey LL65 2LP, tel. 01407 760195

Materials for re-proofing:

Nikwax Ltd
Durgates Industrial Estate, Wadhurst, East Sussex TH5 6DF
Grangers
Grange Close, Clover Nook Industrial Park, Alfreton, Derbyshire DE55 4QT
A useful repair material for small holes and tears is spinnaker tape, which may be available from outdoor shops such as **Tiso** or from ship chandlers.

INDEX

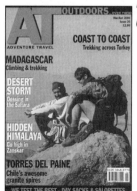

LISTING OF CICERONE GUIDES

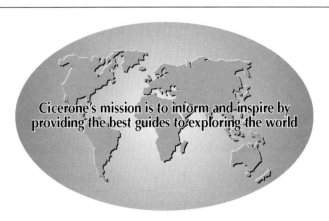

Cicerone's mission is to inform and inspire by providing the best guides to exploring the world

Since its foundation over 30 years ago, Cicerone has specialised in publishing guidebooks and has built a reputation for quality and reliability. It now publishes nearly 300 guides to the major destinations for outdoor enthusiasts, including Europe, UK and the rest of the world.

Written by leading and committed specialists, Cicerone guides are recognised as the most authoritative. They are full of information, maps and illustrations so that the user can plan and complete a successful and safe trip or expedition – be it a long face climb, a walk over Lakeland fells, an alpine traverse, a Himalayan trek or a ramble in the countryside.

With a thorough introduction to assist planning, clear diagrams, maps and colour photographs to illustrate the terrain and route, and accurate and detailed text, Cicerone guides are designed for ease of use and access to the information.

If the facts on the ground change, or there is any aspect of a guide that you think we can improve, we are always delighted to hear from you.

Cicerone Press
2 Police Square Milnthorpe Cumbria LA7 7PY
Tel:01539 562 069   Fax:01539 563 417
e-mail:info@cicerone.co.uk   web:www.cicerone.co.uk

CICERONE